T0114818

GRADE 4

ENGAGE THE BRAIN GAMES

MARCIA L. TATE

CORWIN PRESS
Classroom

For information:

Corwin Press
A SAGE Company
2455 Teller Road
Thousand Oaks, California 91320
CorwinPress.com

SAGE, Ltd.
1 Oliver's Yard
55 City Road
London EC1Y 1SP
United Kingdom

SAGE India Pvt. Ltd.
B 1/I 1 Mohan Cooperative
Industrial Area
Mathura Road, New Delhi
India 110 044

SAGE Asia-Pacific Pvt. Ltd.
33 Pekin Street #02-01
Far East Square
Singapore 048763

ISBN: 978-1-4129-5929-2

This book is printed on acid-free paper.

08 09 10 11 12 10 9 8 7 6 5 4 3 2 1

Executive Editor: Kathleen Hex
Managing Developmental Editor: Christine Hood
Editorial Assistant: Anne O'Dell
Developmental Writers: Nancy and Jeff Sanders
Developmental Editor: Susan Hodges
Proofreader: Mary Barbosa
Art Director: Anthony D. Paular
Design Project Manager: Jeffrey Stith
Cover Designers: Lisa Miller and Monique Hahn
Illustrator: Ann Iosa
Cover Illustrator: Jane Yamada
Design Consultant: The Development Source

TABLE OF CONTENTS

Connections to Standards

This chart shows the national academic standards covered in each chapter.

LANGUAGE ARTS	Standards are covered on pages
Apply a wide range of strategies to comprehend, interpret, evaluate, and appreciate texts. Draw on prior experience, interactions with other readers and writers, knowledge of word meaning and of other texts, word identification strategies, and understanding of textual features (e.g., sound–letter correspondence, sentence structure, context, graphics).	9, 15, 17, 27
Adjust the use of spoken, written, and visual language (e.g., conventions, style, vocabulary) to communicate effectively with a variety of audiences and for different purposes.	21, 23
Apply knowledge of language structure, language conventions (e.g., spelling and punctuation), media techniques, figurative language, and genre to create, critique, and discuss print and nonprint texts.	15
Use spoken, written, and visual language to accomplish a purpose (e.g., for learning, enjoyment, persuasion, and the exchange of information).	9, 15, 23

MATHEMATICS	Standards are covered on pages
Number and Operations—Understand numbers, ways of representing numbers, relationships among numbers, and number systems.	37
Number and Operations—Compute fluently and make reasonable estimates.	29
Geometry—Analyze characteristics and properties of two- and three-dimensional geometric shapes, and develop mathematical arguments about geometric relationships.	31
Geometry—Specify locations and describe spatial relationships using coordinate geometry and other representational systems.	41
Measurement—Apply appropriate techniques, tools, and formulas to determine measurements.	35
Data Analysis and Probability—Understand and apply basic concepts of probability.	44

978-1-4129-5929-2

SCIENCE	Standards are covered on pages
Physical Science—Understand properties of objects and materials.	55
Physical Science—Understand light, heat, electricity, and magnetism.	59, 61
Life Science—Understand organisms and environments.	47, 48
Earth and Space Science—Understand changes in the earth and sky.	50

SOCIAL STUDIES	Standards are covered on pages
Understand culture and cultural diversity.	64, 78
Understand the ways human beings view themselves in and over time.	64
Understand the interactions among people, places, and environments.	70
Understand how people create and change structures of power, authority, and governance.	66
Understand how people organize for the production, distribution, and consumption of goods and services.	73, 76

Introduction

Think back to your years as a student. Which classes do you remember most clearly? Many of us fondly remember those dynamic classes that engaged our attention. However, we can just as easily remember those classes in which lectures seemed endless. The difference is that we can usually recall something we *learned* in the dynamic classroom. This is because our brains were engaged.

Studies confirm what good teachers already know—students who are actively engaged in the learning process absorb more information. Human play fulfills the body's need to express emotions, to bond with others socially, and to explore new learning with challenge, feedback, and success (Beyers, 1998).

Using technological methods, including PET scans and CAT scans, scientists have identified which learning strategies best engage the brain (Tate, 2003). The results reveal that the use of games to energize and engross students is one of the best strategies to activate learning. You might question whether students can truly learn content while playing games. Walk by a classroom where students are playing a game and you might see chaos at first glance. Look again—this is actually collaboration. Amidst the laughter and buzz of competition, students are willingly discussing material from lessons once considered bland. When students are allowed to "play," they interact using all of their senses, stimulating brain function that helps retain content.

How to Use This Book

Correlated with the national standards, this book provides a collection of games that will engage all students, even reluctant learners. The games review concepts in language arts, math, science, social studies, physical education, art, and music, and they follow a format that promotes learning and retention, including focus activity, modeling, guided practice, check for understanding, closing, and independent practice. Using these strategies ensures that students are active participants in their own learning, not passive bystanders.

Each step-by-step activity provides a game that students can use to reinforce learning. Students will enjoy playing variations of classic games such as: Old Maid, Battleship®, Twister®, Pictionary®, Bingo, memory matching, and more!

These brain-compatible activities are sure to engage and motivate every student's brain in your classroom! Watch students progress from passive to active learners as they process competitive, exciting games into learning that is not only fun, but remembered for a lifetime.

Put It Into Practice

Lecture and repetitive worksheets have long been the traditional method of delivering knowledge and reinforcing learning. While some higher-achieving students may engage in this type of learning, educators now know that actively engaging students' brains is not a luxury, but a necessity if students are truly to acquire and retain content, not only for tests but for life.

The 1990s were dubbed the Decade of the Brain because millions of dollars were spent on brain research. Educators today should know more about how students learn than ever before. Learning styles theories that call for student engagement have been proposed for decades, as evidenced by research such as Howard Gardner's theory of multiple intelligences (1983), Bernice McCarthy's 4MAT Model (1990), and VAKT (visual, auditory, kinesthetic, tactile) learning styles theories.

I have identified 20 strategies that, according to brain research and learning styles theories, appear to correlate with the way the brain learns best. I have observed hundreds of teachers—regular education, special education, and gifted. Regardless of the classification or grade level of the students, exemplary teachers consistently use these 20 strategies to deliver memorable classroom instruction and help their students understand and retain vast amounts of content.

These 20 brain-based instructional strategies include the following:

1. Brainstorming and Discussion

2. Drawing and Artwork

3. Field Trips

4. Games

5. Graphic Organizers, Semantic Maps, and Word Webs

6. Humor

7. Manipulatives, Experiments, Labs, and Models

8. Metaphors, Analogies, and Similes

9. Mnemonic Devices

10. Movement

11. Music, Rhythm, Rhyme, and Rap

12. Project-based and Problem-based Instruction

13. Reciprocal Teaching and Cooperative Learning

14. Role Play, Drama, Pantomime, Charades

15. Storytelling

16. Technology

17. Visualization and Guided Imagery

18. Visuals

19. Work Study and Apprenticeships

20. Writing and Journals

This book features Instructional Strategy 4: Games. Through play, people fulfill the body's need to express emotions, to bond with others socially, and to explore new learning with challenge, feedback, and success (Beyers, 1998). In addition, when students are given the opportunity to redesign a game with which they are already familiar, such as Bingo, brain connections are made for a better understanding of the alternate content (Jensen, 1995).

Games involve active learning. They motivate students by making learning fun and engaging. In today's fast-paced world, students are frequently asked to change gears quickly, jumping from one activity to another, sometimes with little time in between to process what they have learned. Using games as a teaching strategy makes sense. Students thrive on the novelty of game playing and the quick action often associated with games. Playing learning games allows students to actively rehearse information they are expected to know in a non-threatening atmosphere. Furthermore, when students are involved in the design and construction of a learning game, the game's effectiveness is enhanced (Wolfe, 2001).

Types of effective learning games include board games, card games, memory games, trivia games, games that encourage physicality, games that involve using the senses, games that involve creative imagination, and many more.

These memorable strategies help students make sense of learning by focusing on the ways the brain learns best. Fully supported by the latest brain research, the games presented in this resource provide the tools you need to boost motivation, energy, and most important, the academic achievement of your students.

CHAPTER 1

Language Arts

My Silly Story

Objective

Students will use context clues and apply a variety of reading strategies to choose a title that supports the main idea, identify the main character and setting in a story, and determine correct story sequence.

Materials

- My Silly Story reproducible
- My Silly Story Cards reproducibles
- index cards (optional)
- book students have recently read
- dice
- resealable plastic bags
- large manila envelopes

All stories contain the same elements (e.g., character, setting, title, beginning, middle, end). These elements are combined in an infinite number of ways to make every story unique. In this game, students will use a variety of reading strategies to identify the main parts of a story.

1. Prepare the game by making one copy of the **My Silly Story reproducible (page 11)** for each student. Make two copies of the **My Silly Story Cards reproducibles (pages 12–14)** for each group of three to six students. Make an extra copy to use as an answer key. If you choose, make additional game cards by writing questions and answers on index cards.

2. Cut out the cards and cut off the answers. On the back of each card, write the number shown on the opposite side (*1* for title cards, *2* for main character cards, and so on). Laminate each set of 36 cards for durability, if desired. Place each set of cards in a resealable plastic bag, and store the bags in large manila envelopes.

3. Show students a copy of a book that they have recently read. Ask questions to help them recall the main elements of the story, such as: *What was the name of this story? Where did it take place? What happened first? Next? Last?*

   Write students' responses on the board, and label them using the following categories: *Title, Character, Setting, Beginning, Middle, End.* Point out that these are the main parts of any story.

4. Tell students that they will play a card game that asks them to identify the six main parts of six different stories. The stories will be mixed up because the cards from the six stories are shuffled together. Each student's cards will form a silly story.

5. Gather a group of three to six players. Give each student a copy of the My Silly Story reproducible. Shuffle the cards and place them facedown in six different piles. All the 1s go in one pile, all the 2s in a second pile, all the 3s in a third pile, and so on.

6. Demonstrate how to play the game. Player 1 rolls the die. The player to his or her left takes the top card from the pile with the corresponding number and reads it aloud. If Player 1 answers correctly, he or she gets one point. If not, no points are awarded. Whether or not the answer is correct, Player 1 keeps the card.

7. It is now Player 2's turn. After rolling the die, the player to the left takes the top card on the corresponding pile and reads it to Player 2, who keeps the card after giving an answer.

8. Play continues around the circle. If players already hold a card with the same number as the number rolled, they skip their turn. The game is over when one player collects all six cards (one from each pile). The player with the most points wins the game. Circulate among students and check to see that they understand the rules. Make sure each group designates one student as the scorekeeper.

9. After the game, the remaining players take turns going around the circle to pick up any leftover cards they still need from the piles. When everyone has all six cards, have them complete their reproducible by writing in the answers from each card in the corresponding section.

10. Provide time for students to read their silly stories aloud to each other. Also, review the cards and discuss the answers with students.

978-1-4129-5929-2

Name _____ Date _____

My Silly Story

Directions: Use your Silly Story Cards to fill in the information below.

1. Title: _____

2. Main Character: _____

    I am a(n) _____

3. Setting: My story takes place _____

_____

_____

Here's my Silly Story

4. Beginning: _____

_____

_____

_____

_____

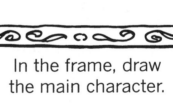

In the frame, draw
the main character.

5. Middle:

  First, _____

  Next, _____

  Last, _____

6. End: _____

_____

_____

_____

My Silly Story Cards

1. TITLE
Pick the best title for the paragraph.
You are an animal at the zoo. One day you found a key and got out of your cage.
a. Cats and Dogs
b. All About Animals
c. One Day at the Zoo

Answer: c

2. MAIN CHARACTER
Who is the main character?
You are an animal from the jungle.
You like to swing in trees.
You like to eat bananas.

Answer: a monkey

3. SETTING
Which best describes the story setting?
a. one day at the zoo
b. my friend's name is Aimee
c. an octopus has eight arms

Answer: a

4. BEGINNING
Which makes the best beginning?
a. Elephants are very big animals.
b. One day, I was sitting in my cage at the zoo.
c. The zoo opens at nine o'clock.

Answer: b

5. MIDDLE
Order the events so the story makes sense:
a. I spotted a key inside my cage.
b. I got out of my cage and ran to the popcorn stand.
c. I got the key and opened the lock.

Answer: a, c, b

6. END
Which makes the best ending?
a. The elephants liked popcorn, too.
b. Giraffes are the zoo's tallest animals.
c. I got popcorn for all my friends. From then on, we had popcorn every night.

Answer: c

1. TITLE
Pick the best title for the paragraph.
The princess saw a unicorn. She asked him for three wishes.
a. The Myth of Unicorns
b. Three Wishes
c. If Horses Could Fly

Answer: b

2. MAIN CHARACTER
Who is the main character?
You are a kind of horse.
You live in a world of make-believe.
You have one horn in the middle of your forehead.

Answer: a unicorn

Reproducible

My Silly Story Cards

3. SETTING **Which best describes the story setting?** a. fairies and dwarfs and gnomes b. candy under the bed c. long ago in a make-believe forest	**4. BEGINNING** **Which makes the best beginning?** a. Once upon a time, a princess lived in a forest with purple trees. b. Trees are tall and green. c. She never returned to the forest again.
Answer: c	*Answer: a*
5. MIDDLE **Order the events so the story makes sense:** a. She wished for beauty, gold, and a handsome prince. b. The princess asked for three wishes. c. The unicorn gave her a frog so her three wishes could come true.	**6. END** **Which makes the best ending?** a. When the princess kissed the frog, she turned into a frog princess. b. Frogs like to catch flies for dinner. c. The princess had to cut off her long red hair.
Answer: b, a, c	*Answer: a*
1. TITLE **Pick the best title for the paragraph.** You are gum stuck on a sidewalk outside a bank. A bank robber steps on you. You make him trip and fall. a. We Bank at Countibank b. The Day I Caught a Bank Robber c. Sidewalks Are Sticky	**2. MAIN CHARACTER** **Who is the main character?** You are sticky and sweet. People like to chew you. Sometimes they use you to blow bubbles.
Answer: b	*Answer: bubble gum*
3. SETTING **Which best describes the story setting?** a. my father was a police officer b. math is my favorite subject c. last week outside a bank	**4. BEGINNING** **Which makes the best beginning?** a. Pink bubble gum tastes the best. b. I was stuck flat on the ground on a sidewalk outside of a bank. c. I am sticky, messy, and stuck to your face.
Answer: c	*Answer: b*

My Silly Story Cards

5. MIDDLE
Order the events so the story makes sense:
a. A bank robber stepped on me, and I got stuck on his shoe.
b. He fell down and got caught.
c. I stretched out like a rubber band, and then he tripped.

Answer: a, c, b

6. END
Which makes the best ending?
a. Then I was famous! They put me in a museum where people admire me.
b. The bank robber had a bag of money.
c. I love to stick to people's shoes.

Answer: a

1. TITLE
Pick the best title for the paragraph.
A giant octopus lived deep in the sea. It spent most of its time guarding a treasure chest in an ocean cave.
a. Guarding the Treasure
b. Under the Sea
c. Spiny Crustaceans

Answer: a

2. MAIN CHARACTER
Who is the main character?
You live in the ocean.
You are not a whale or a shark.
You have eight arms.

Answer: an octopus

3. SETTING
Which best describes the story setting?
a. sharks have a lot of sharp teeth
b. this morning inside a pretty underwater cave
c. the octopus woke up in a fright

Answer: b

4. BEGINNING
Which makes the best beginning?
a. It all started this morning by a cave under the sea.
b. How many whales can you name?
c. The Atlantic Ocean has cold water.

Answer: a

5. MIDDLE
Order the events so the story makes sense:
a. A pirate saw the octopus guarding the treasure chest.
b. The octopus squirted a purple cloud of ink to confuse the pirate.
c. An octopus found a treasure chest.

Answer: c, a, b

6. END
Which makes the best ending?
a. The pirate tried to grab the treasure.
b. The octopus grabbed the treasure chest and swam away to a new cave.
c. Treasure chests are filled with jewels.

Answer: b

 978-1-4129-5929-2 • © Corwin Press

Mystery Word

Objective
Students will practice spelling skills.

Materials
- lists of spelling words
- crayons
- 12" x 18" construction paper
- 3" x 5" index cards
- resealable plastic bags

Finding creative ways of practicing for a spelling test can spark enthusiasm in even your most reluctant learners. In this game, students choose one word from their spelling list and secretly spell it out with individual alphabet letters written on index cards. They then pair up with a partner to play a "mystery word" guessing game.

1. Have students practice writing the spelling words from their list five times each, using a different-colored crayon each time. When they are done, tell them that they will play a game to help practice their spelling words.

2. Pair up students and have partners sit on opposite sides of a desk, facing each other. Give each student a piece of construction paper and a stack of about 20 index cards. Instruct students to each choose a word from their spelling list. Encourage them to choose a word that they have struggled with in the past. This will be their "mystery word."

3. Demonstrate how to write the mystery word on index cards, one letter per card, being careful not to let anyone see. Place the letters of the word facedown in left-to-right order on a sheet of construction paper. Explain that players may add up to five blank index cards on either side of their word to try to trick their partner. When the mystery words are ready, players carefully rotate the construction paper to face their partner.

4. Show students how to play the game. As students watch, sit down to play with a partner. Set out cards to spell your own mystery word while your partner does the same. Then ask questions to guess your partner's word. For example: *Do you have an e?* If your partner has an e, he or she turns over the card to reveal that letter. (The player may peek at each card before turning over the correct one.) If there are two or more cards with that letter, only one letter is revealed.

5. Whether or not your guess was correct, it is now your partner's turn. Your partner now asks if your word contains a specific letter. Play continues back and forth. The first person to correctly guess the other player's mystery word wins the game.

6. A player may try to guess the entire word on his or her turn by asking a question such as: *Is your word* **field**? If the guess is correct, the player must also guess the correct spelling of the word. If the guess is incorrect, however, the player automatically loses the game. If players discover at the end of the game that one of the words is spelled incorrectly, that player automatically loses the game.

7. Check to see that everyone understands how to play the game. Then provide time for students to play with partners. When finished with one game, have them switch partners and choose a new mystery word from their spelling list to play again. Letter cards from the first round may be reused in later rounds. New letters may be added by writing on blank index cards.

8. After the game, provide resealable plastic bags for students to store their letter cards. Go around the room and have students use one of their mystery words in a sentence.

Extended Learning

Ask partners to give each other a practice spelling test. Encourage students to add misspelled words to their list to use as new mystery words in future games.

978-1-4129-5929-2

Spoon Up a Sentence

Objective

Students will practice joining a subject and a predicate to make a complete sentence.

Materials
- Spoon Up a Sentence: Game Cards reproducibles
- cardstock
- scissors
- plastic spoons

In this fast-paced card game, students will practice joining subjects and predicates together to make silly sentences.

1. Prepare for the game by reproducing the **Spoon Up a Sentence: Game Cards reproducibles (pages 19–20)** on cardstock. Laminate and cut out the cards.

2. Review the parts of a sentence as well as capitalization and punctuation rules: *The subject tells **who** or **what**. The predicate tells **what happened**. Sentences always start with a capital letter and end with a punctuation mark.* Explain that a complete sentence must have both a subject and a predicate. Write two lists on the board, one for subjects and one for predicates. Ask for suggestions for each list.

3. Draw two large speech bubbles on the board. Invite two volunteers to come to the board. Give a silly dialogue prompt, for example: *The lizard said; An elephant thought; The monkey shouted.* Instruct the two students to each choose one subject and one predicate from the lists and write a silly complete sentence in their speech bubbles. Continue the activity until every student has a turn at the board.

4. Explain to students that they will play a card game in which they collect four cards that form a complete sentence. Divide the class into groups of four, and have each group sit in a circle. Place three plastic spoons in the center of each group, and then demonstrate how to play the game.

5. The goal is to collect four cards that make a complete sentence. Two cards form the subject (e.g., *A loud* and *parrot*) and two cards form the predicate (e.g., *flew* and *in the sky*). The sentence can be silly and nonsensical, but it must start with a capital letter, have a subject and a predicate, and end with a period. Show four of the cards together to demonstrate what the completed sentence looks like, to make sure all students understand how to play the game.

6. One player shuffles the cards and deals four cards to each player. Players should immediately examine their cards. All players then simultaneously place one card facedown to their left and pick up the card that was placed to their right. Players continue passing cards quickly in this manner until one player realizes he or she is holding four cards that make a complete sentence. Without saying anything, that player grabs a spoon.

7. As soon as other players realize someone has taken a spoon, they try to grab a spoon, too. The player without a spoon loses that round. To score one point, the winner must place his or her cards faceup, identify the subject and predicate, and read the complete sentence. The first player to get five points wins the game.

8. After the game, ask students to identify two or three sentences in a favorite book. Allow time to share sentences, and have students identify the subjects and predicates.

Extended Learning

Invite students to pair up with partners. One student writes a list of subjects numbered *1–5*. Without seeing his or her partner's list, the other student writes a list of predicates numbered *1–5*. Partners then read their corresponding subjects and predicates together, creating silly sentences.

978-1-4129-5929-2

Spoon Up a Sentence: Game Cards

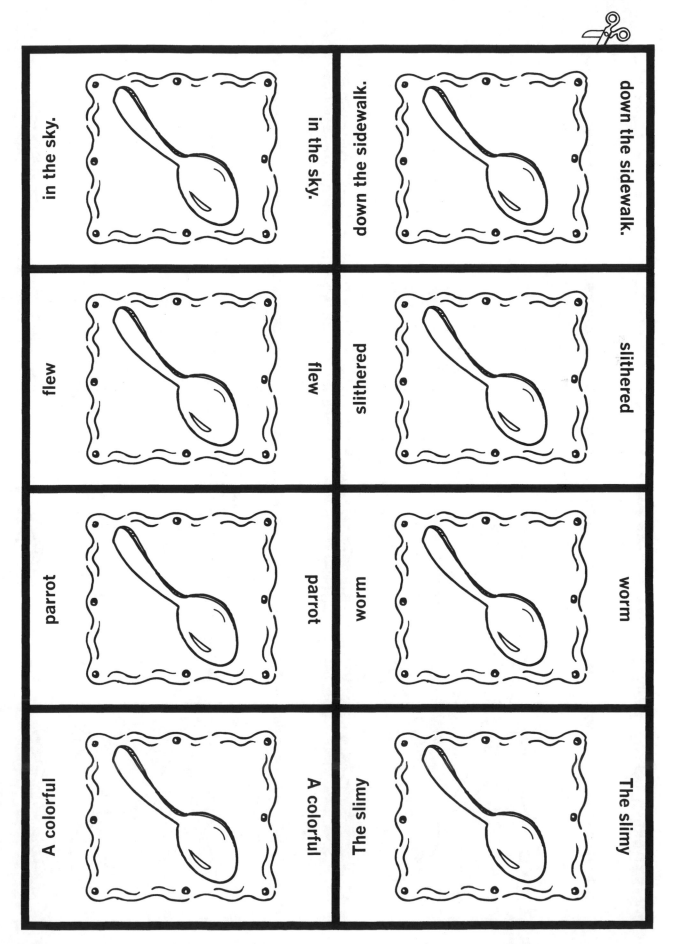

in the sky.

in the sky.

down the sidewalk.

down the sidewalk.

flew

flew

slithered

slithered

parrot

parrot

worm

worm

A colorful

A colorful

The slimy

The slimy

Spoon Up a Sentence: Game Cards

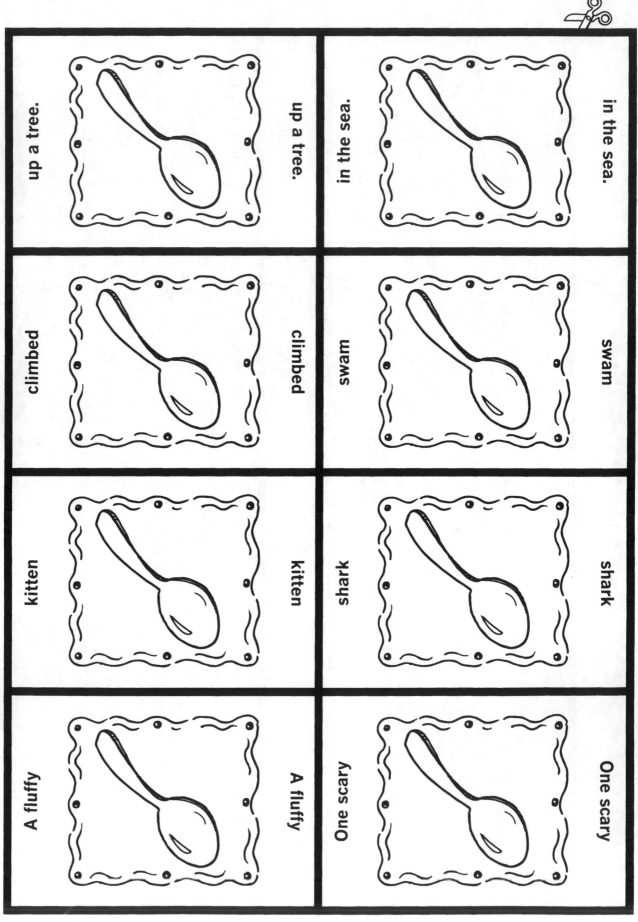

up a tree.

up a tree.

climbed

climbed

kitten

kitten

A fluffy

A fluffy

in the sea.

in the sea.

swam

swam

shark

shark

One scary

One scary

978-1-4129-5929-2 • © Corwin Press

Describe It!

Objective
Students will identify and use adjectives to describe nouns.

Materials
- sticky notes
- three objects of different sizes (e.g., book, pencil, eraser)

Identifying and learning to use adjectives can help make students' writing more colorful, precise, and interesting. Adjectives also give students concrete tools to better express themselves. In this game, students provide adjective clues to help their team guess various words.

1. List several nouns on the board. Remind students that a noun is a word that names a person, a place, or a thing. Explain that an adjective describes a noun. An adjective can tell what kind or how many. List several adjectives on the board. Ask volunteers to suggest adjectives that describe what kind or how many (e.g., *orange, small, new, three, many, few*).

2. Hold up three objects of different sizes, such as a book, a pencil, and an eraser. Tell students: *Adjectives can be used to compare things and tell how they are alike or different.* Ask how the three objects compare in size. For example: *The pencil is **bigger** than the eraser. The book is the **biggest** of all. The eraser is the **smallest** of all.* Ask volunteers to suggest adjectives that compare to add to the list (e.g., *wider, widest, tall, tallest, tiny, tiniest*).

3. Add *more* and *most* to the list. Explain that longer adjectives use the word *more* or *most* to compare. For example: *A governor is **more important** than a mayor. The president is the **most important** leader of all.* Point out that we do not say *importanter* or *importantest.*

4. Inform students that they will play a game wherein each team tries to guess a word by hearing clues (adjectives) that describe the word. Divide the class into two teams. Choose one volunteer from each team to come to the front of the room. Write the same noun on two sticky notes and give each volunteer one of the notes. Do not let students show the word to their teammates. (You may wish to write several nouns on index cards ahead of time for students to draw randomly out of a hat or bag.)

5. Demonstrate how to play the game. Have the first volunteer say either an adjective describing the noun or a word associated with the noun. Each time a player uses an adjective for a clue, the team earns an extra point. For example, if the word is *elephant*, the student might say *gray*. Since this clue is an adjective, the team earns an extra point. The first team gets one guess based on the

student's clue (only one player guesses per turn). If the guess is incorrect, the other team gets a chance.

6. The second volunteer might say *Africa*. Since the clue is not an adjective, no extra point is earned. The first player on the second team then tries to guess the word. If the guess is incorrect, it is the first team's turn again.

7. The first volunteer might then say *heaviest*. Check to see that students understand how an extra point is scored because the clue is an adjective. Play continues with alternating players until someone guesses the correct word. The team who guesses the correct word earns five points. The player who guesses the word then goes to the front of the room and starts with a new noun. The team with the most points after a given number of rounds wins the game.

8. After the game, invite students to illustrate one of the nouns used for the game. Instruct them to write several sentences using adjectives to describe the person, place, or thing.

Gotcha!

Objective

Students will choose an adverb to modify a verb.

When students can identify and generate strong verbs and adverbs, their writing becomes more evocative. They learn to show, not tell. In this game, students quickly choose one verb and one adverb from a cube that they pass around a circle.

1. To prepare for this game, make several game cubes, one for each group of eight to ten students. Photocopy the **Gotcha! Game Cube reproducibles (pages 25–26)** for each cube. To make a game cube, wrap an empty facial tissue box in a piece of gift wrap or butcher paper. Then glue one square from the reproducibles on each side of the box so that all the sides are covered (three verb squares and three adverb squares).

2. Write a list of verbs on the board. Explain that action verbs tell what the action is (e.g., *grow, stand, mix, jumped, sat*). Include common helping verbs in the list as well (e.g., *am, is, are, was, were, will, has, have, had*).

3. Tell students: *Adverbs can tell **how**, **when**, or **where**.* Write three lists of adverbs on the board. For example: *How—quickly, slowly, happily, sadly, loudly, softly. When—never, soon, often, once, always. Where—inside, outside, off, downstairs, upstairs, there.* Explain that adverbs usually describe verbs.

4. Divide the class into groups of eight to ten students and have each group sit in a circle on the floor. Give one game cube to each group. Demonstrate how to look at the cube and say aloud one verb and one adverb that go together and make sense (e.g., *jumped inside, never stand, sat there*). Explain that an adverb can come before or after a verb.

5. To make sure students understand how the game works, ask a volunteer from each group to choose a verb and an adverb from the cube.

Jumped inside!

6. Set a timer for one minute or less. Instruct each group to pass the cube from student to student around the circle, each one choosing a verb and an adverb to say aloud before passing it on. When the timer rings, everyone shouts: *Gotcha!* The student holding the game cube must then leave the circle.

7. The student from the first circle takes the place of the student from the second circle, who takes the place of the student from the third circle, and so on, so they can all join in for the next round. Play continues for as many rounds as desired.

8. If you wish, increase the competition level by having a playoff round. Once a student is caught holding a game cube, he or she is out of the game. The last student in each circle then joins the other winners to make a new circle. Invite these students to participate in a playoff round.

9. After the game, give each student a turn to hold the cube and say a complete sentence that contains a verb and an adverb. Make sure the verb and adverb make sense together and are used correctly in the sentence.

Extended Learning
To increase the challenge of the game, require that students say an entire sentence using the adverb and verb before passing the cube.

Gotcha! Game Cube: Verbs

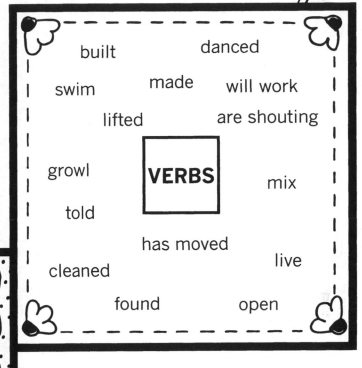

built
danced
swim
made
will work
lifted
are shouting
growl
VERBS
mix
told
has moved
live
cleaned
found
open

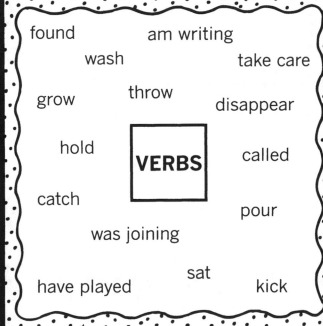

found
am writing
wash
take care
grow
throw
disappear
hold
VERBS
called
catch
pour
was joining
sat
have played
kick

hide
dive
stand
had read
jumped
remember
hit
sleep
VERBS
tripped
read
climb
were laughing
tell
drop
is running

Gotcha! Game Cube: Adverbs

then   sometimes   now
never   once   finally
first   **ADVERBS When?**   always
after
next
forever
again   before
often   soon

quickly   excitedly   happily
skillfully   poorly   gracefully
proudly   **ADVERBS How?**   softly
loudly   fast
sadly
brightly   slowly
carefully   patiently

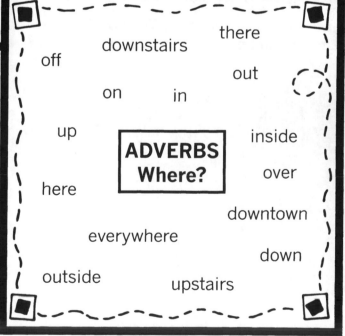

there
off   downstairs   out
on   in
up   **ADVERBS Where?**   inside
over
here
downtown
everywhere   down
outside   upstairs

Jump and Spell

Objective
Students will review rules for capitalization.

Materials
- 1" graph paper
- jump ropes

Learning grammar and punctuation rules is easier to do with a catchy rhyme. By reciting this jump-rope rhyme students will remember to capitalize proper nouns.

1. Review rules for capitalizing the names of people, places, and things. Include initials or titles used for a person's name, such as *Dr.*, *Mr.*, and *Mrs*. Give each student a piece of graph paper and explain that they will be making word searches with proper nouns.

2. Ask students to identify common groups of proper nouns such as holidays, people, oceans, parks, and streets. Encourage them to brainstorm other proper nouns (e.g., *Uncle Alan, Shasta Avenue, New Year's Day*). Write students' suggestions on the board. Instruct students to write the word or words on their graph paper. (Remind them to skip a space between multiple words.) Check to make sure that students are using uppercase and lowercase letters.

3. When students are done adding words to their word search, tell them to fill in the blank spaces with random lowercase letters. Then have them trade word searches with a partner and circle each other's words, using the list on the board as a guide.

4. Tell students that they will learn a jump-rope rhyme to help them remember the rules about capitalizing proper nouns. Teach them the following rhyme:

   Proper nouns are fun to spell.
   Each one starts with a capital.
   Dr., Mr., Mrs., Miss,
   Days and months are on the list.
   States and cities. Spell a few.
   His name. Her name. My name, too!
   Jump and spell. Do you know how?
   *Why don't you spell **(name)** now?*

5. Distribute jump ropes to students and demonstrate how to use the jump-rope rhyme. First, choose one proper noun to spell. Then recite the rhyme, substituting a proper name in the blank. Students then finish spelling the word aloud, jumping once for each letter (e.g., *capital C-a-s-e-y*). Have groups choose their own words and take turns with the jump rope. As students jump and spell, check to see that they are using capital letters correctly.

6. After all students have had a chance to use the jump-rope rhyme and to spell proper nouns, ask them to share what they learned about the rules for capitalization.

Extended Learning

- Instruct students to "read the room" to locate proper and common nouns in the classroom. These can be found on maps, the class roster, posters, and schoolwork mounted on the walls.

- Invite students to write proper nouns in their journals for all the people and places they know in their daily lives, and use those words in sentences. For example: *Dr. Chang takes care of my teeth. Mr. Gomez delivers our mail. My family lives next door to Mr. and Mrs. Hodges. I live on Red Oak Avenue. My favorite restaurant is Silver Spur Steakhouse.*

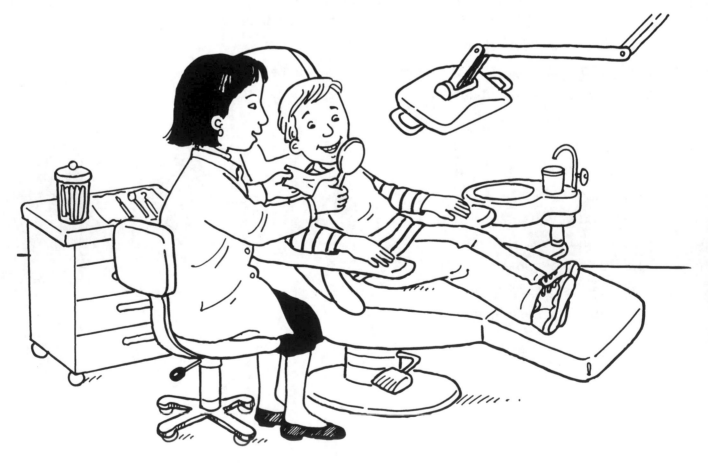

CHAPTER 2

Mathematics

Simon Says Math

Objective

Students will use mental math to practice computation.

Materials
- deck of playing cards (with face cards removed)

Students love to play Simon Says! Combine this action-packed game with mental math to add instant pizzazz to math lessons. This game is easily adapted for addition, subtraction, or multiplication.

1. Review math facts with a deck of cards. Remove the face cards and use only the numbers *1–10*. Deal two cards to each student. Instruct students to add, subtract, or multiply the two numbers using mental math and give you the answer. (Division will work only with certain number combinations.) Move from one student to the next until they all have a chance to respond.

2. Tell students that they will play a mental math game to help them practice addition and subtraction facts. You will ask them to compute math problems in their head while following the basic rules of Simon Says. For example: *If Simon says to perform an action, or add or subtract a number, you must do it. If Simon does not say it, do not do it.*

3. Demonstrate how to play the game. Have all students stand at their desks. Start by saying something like:

   Simon says, "Put your right hand in the air."
   (Students raise their right hands.)
   Simon says, "Add 5 plus 3."
   Simon says, "Put your hand down."
   (Students lower their hands.)
   Hop up and down.
   (Students should stand still. Anyone who hops must sit down.)
   Simon says, "Add 4 plus 8."
   Simon says, "Give me the answer."
   (Students should hold up fingers to indicate the answer *12*. If their answer is incorrect, they sit down.)

4. Show students how to hold up one finger on the left hand for the tens and hold up two fingers on the right hand for ones. Make sure the ones digit in two-digit answers is not more than five so students can show you the answer by holding up their fingers.

5. Check to see that students understand how to show the answers using their fingers. Continue playing the game. Students sitting at their desks should also compute the mental math problems and show the answers using their fingers. Occasionally say: *Simon says everyone with the correct answer is back in the game.* Play the game as long as you want. Students still standing at the end of the game are the winners.

6. After the game, divide the class into pairs and have them quiz each other on math facts. You may also invite students to lead the class in another game of Simon Says Math.

978-1-4129-5929-2

Monster Math

Objective

Students will review the definitions of geometric shapes and solids and identify corresponding models.

Stop signs, cardboard boxes, ice-cream cones—almost everywhere students look, they can see geometric shapes. As students' math knowledge develops, so does their understanding of the properties and definitions of geometric shapes and solids. In this game, students match the name of each shape and solid with its corresponding picture.

Materials
- Monster Math Game Cards reproducibles
- cardstock
- glue
- construction paper
- rulers
- scissors
- tape

1. Create a set of cards by reproducing the **Monster Math Game Cards reproducibles (pages 33–34)** on cardstock. Cut out the cards and laminate them for durability if you wish.

2. Review the name and attributes of each shape and solid represented on the cards. Ask students to point out or name other objects that represent various geometric shapes and solids. For example: *book—rectangular prism; dice—cubes; stop sign—octagon; yield sign—triangle.* Discuss terms such as *face, edge,* and *vertex.* Demonstrate how to distinguish between geometric solids by determining the number and shape of faces, edges, and vertices.

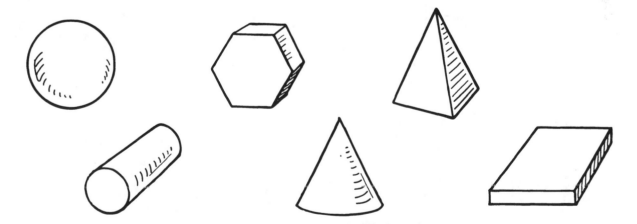

3. Tell students they will play a card game similar to Old Maid to practice identifying geometric shapes and solids. A group of three or four students may play at a time. Show students how to play the game. Shuffle the cards and deal all of them among the players. (Some players will have an extra card.) Players should immediately discard any matches they already hold in their hand. Check that correct matches are made.

4. The dealer goes first and picks one card at random from the hand of the player to the left. If the card matches a card in the dealer's hand, he or she discards the matching pair. The player to the left then takes a turn and picks one card at random from the player to his or her left. Play continues around the group until all matches are discarded. The player left holding the Math Monster card loses the game.

5. Invite students to play in small groups. Circulate around the room as they play, and assist as needed. Make sure students are making correct matches, and act as "judge" if there is a dispute in any of the games.

6. After the game, challenge students to use construction paper, scissors, rulers, and tape to make two paper models each—one geometric shape, such as a triangle, and one solid shape, such as a cone. Allow time for students to share their models.

Monster Math Game Cards

circle	(circle shape)	hexagon	(hexagon shape)
triangle	(triangle shape)	octagon	(octagon shape)
square	(square shape)	parallelogram	(parallelogram shape)
rectangle	(rectangle shape)	rhombus	(rhombus shape)
pentagon	(pentagon shape)	trapezoid	(trapezoid shape)

Monster Math Game Cards

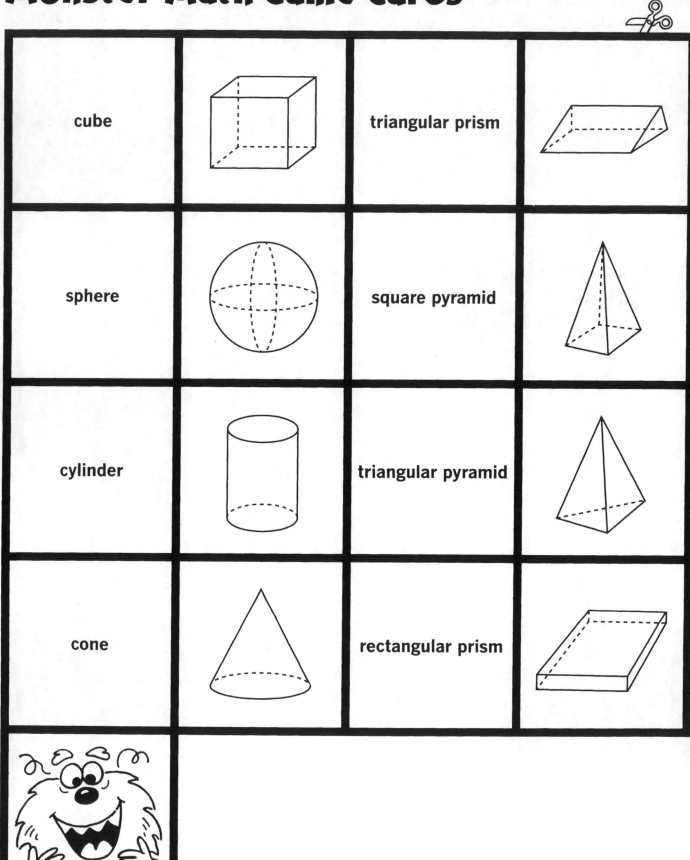

cube		triangular prism	
sphere		square pyramid	
cylinder		triangular pyramid	
cone		rectangular prism	

Reproducible

I Spot Metrics

Objective
Students will measure objects with a metric ruler.

Counting by tens is a snap with metrics. In this guessing game, students measure objects in the classroom with metric rulers, write down their measurements, and then try to guess which objects their classmates measured.

Materials
- metric rulers
- meter stick

1. Distribute metric rulers to students. Count the millimeter marks on the ruler aloud together and show students that there are ten millimeters in one centimeter. Count the centimeters aloud together up to ten. Explain that there are ten centimeters in one decimeter. Hold up a meter stick. Show students that there are ten decimeters in one meter, and point out that there are 1,000 meters in one kilometer.

2. Demonstrate how to measure a few objects, such as a pencil, a shoe, or the edge of a desk. On the board, write the name of each object you measure and record its measurement to the nearest centimeter. Have students write the name of each object on a piece of paper and record its measurement to the nearest centimeter. Check that students know how to measure an object and record the measurement.

3. Pair up students and instruct them to find five to ten objects in plain view in the classroom that they want to measure. (The objects cannot be hidden inside a backpack or underneath a stack of books because everyone needs to see them clearly to play the game.) Have students use their metric rulers to measure each object. Remind them to write the name of each object and its measurement.

4. After students finish collecting measurements, demonstrate how to play the game. Invite a pair of students to stand at the front of the room. Tell them to choose one object from their list, such as a pencil that is 14 centimeters long. Remind them that the object must be in plain view. One student then announces: *I spot something that measures 14 centimeters.*

5. Students take turns guessing the object until the correct object is named. If someone guesses: *Is it a pencil?* students still have to continue guessing until they locate which pencil it is. The student who guesses correctly then comes to the front of the room with his or her partner. They choose one object from their list, such as

a book that is 28 centimeters. One of them then announces: *I spot something that measures 28 centimeters.*

6. Students who are trying to guess may ask for clues about in which part of the room the object is located. For example: *Is it on the wall? Is it touching the ground? Is it on a desk?* If nobody can guess the correct object, the pair gets to choose a second object from their list for classmates to guess.

7. After the game, invite students to share which objects they measured and what their measurements were.

Extended Learning

Encourage students to take home their metric rulers to measure items around their homes. Have them list the objects' names and measurements. The next day, invite students to challenge each other to see if they can guess the objects. For example: *In my bedroom, I measured something 75 centimeters high.* (Guesses might include *desk, bed, window frame,* and so on.)

Fraction Match

Objective

Students will match pictures of improper fractions with mixed numbers.

Materials
• Fraction Match Game Cards reproducibles

This simple matching game helps students to review the concepts of improper fractions and mixed numbers. As they play, it will also become easier for them to visualize improper fractions and learn how to write them as mixed numbers.

1. Reproduce the **Fraction Match Game Cards reproducibles (pages 39–40)**. Cut out a set of cards for each group of three to four students.

2. Review with students how an improper fraction can be written as a mixed number. Draw a picture of 7/3 using three circles divided into thirds. Shade in the first two circles completely and shade in 1/3 of the last circle. Write *2 1/3* next to the picture. Explain that a mixed number is made up of a whole number and a fraction. Show other examples of improper fractions and mixed numbers.

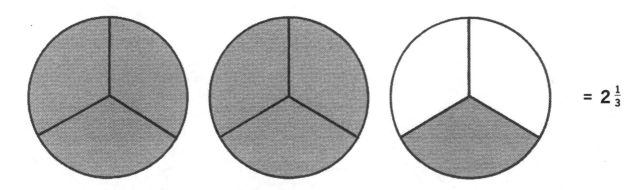

$$= 2\tfrac{1}{3}$$

3. Tell students that they will play a simple matching game. The object of the game is to use their knowledge of fractions as well as their memories to match pictures of improper fractions with mixed numbers.

4. Divide the class into groups of three or four. Give each group a set of 48 Fraction Match game cards. Instruct them to mix up the cards and place them facedown in a "grid" format on a desk.

5. Model how to play the game with a volunteer. The first player turns over two cards. If the cards show the same value (match), the player keeps the pair and takes another turn. If the values do not match, the player turns the cards back over in the same positions, and the next player takes a turn. Emphasize to students that part of the challenge is remembering where they see certain pictures or fractions so they can make matches later in the game.

6. Players continue to take turns until all the matches are found. The player with the most matches wins the game.

7. After the game, ask students to explain the difference between a fraction and a mixed number. Invite volunteers to demonstrate their explanations on the board.

Extended Learning

Hold a pizza party with the class. Start with three or more whole pizzas. As you slice and serve the pizzas, pause to let students name different quantities of pizza using fractions and mixed numbers. For example: *Jason ate 1/8 of a pizza. The girls ate 1 6/8 pizzas. There are 2 2/8 pizzas left.*

Fraction Match Game Cards

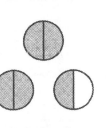	$3\frac{1}{3}$	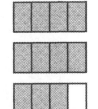	$2\frac{3}{4}$
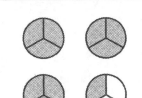	$1\frac{3}{4}$	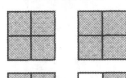	$3\frac{2}{4}$
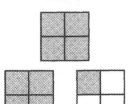	$2\frac{1}{4}$		$1\frac{2}{3}$
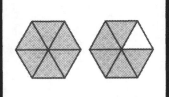	$1\frac{5}{6}$	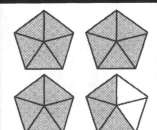	$3\frac{3}{5}$
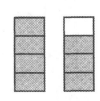	$2\frac{1}{2}$		$2\frac{1}{6}$
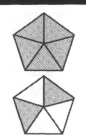	$1\frac{2}{5}$	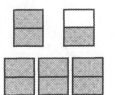	$4\frac{1}{2}$

Fraction Match Game Cards

(three squares, each divided in halves, shaded)	$2\frac{2}{3}$	(two pentagons, one shaded, one partly shaded)	$1\frac{1}{5}$
(four circles divided in halves, shaded)	$3\frac{1}{2}$	(three circles divided in thirds, shaded)	$2\frac{1}{3}$
(three pentagons divided in fifths, shaded)	$2\frac{4}{5}$	(four circles divided in thirds, shaded)	$3\frac{2}{3}$
(two rectangles divided in fifths, shaded)	$1\frac{1}{4}$	(three pentagons, two shaded, one partly shaded)	$2\frac{1}{5}$
(four hexagons divided in sixths, shaded)	$3\frac{5}{6}$	(two circles divided in thirds, shaded)	$1\frac{1}{3}$
(three pentagons, two shaded, one partly shaded)	$2\frac{3}{5}$	(two hexagons divided in sixths, one shaded, one partly shaded)	$1\frac{3}{6}$

Reproducible

Sink It!

Objective

Students will plot points on a graph and name the ordered pairs.

Students of all ages enjoy a good game of hide-and-seek! They will be eager to practice naming point coordinates in this paper-and-pencil variation of the classic board game *Battleship®* (a registered trademark of Hasbro, Inc.).

Materials
- Sink It! Game Grids reproducible
- overhead projector and transparency
- file folders
- tape

1. To prepare for the game, reproduce the **Sink It! Game Grids reproducible (page 43)** on an overhead transparency, and give each student a photocopy. Display the transparency for the class. Mark the point *(3,2)* on the coordinate grid.

2. Demonstrate how to find the ordered pair of that point. Say: *Start at 0. Move right three units. Move up two units. The ordered pair for this point is (3,2).* Tell students that they will be playing a game to practice naming ordered pairs of points they plot on a graph.

3. Explain that students will plot points for five different ships: a tugboat, a sailboat, a yacht, a submarine, and a destroyer. They will try to find and sink their opponent's ships. The first ship, a tugboat, is a single point *(3,2)*. Show them how to plot a sailboat with two points, a yacht with three points, a submarine with four points, and a destroyer with five points. Write the coordinates (ordered pairs) for the points of each ship.

4. Instruct students to plot five ships on the grid labeled *My Coordinate Grid*, as shown on the example below. Remind them to plot their ships on different points of the grid. The ships can be plotted vertically, horizontally, or diagonally. Have them write the ordered pairs of each point. As they work, walk through the room to check for comprehension and accuracy.

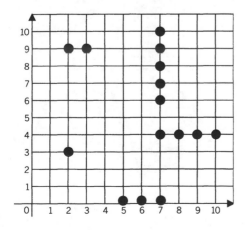

5. When students are ready, have them pair up with partners. Give each student a file folder, so they can hide their coordinate grid inside as they play. Or, students can prop up the paper folder between them to avoid peeking at their partner's grid.

6. Demonstrate how to play the game. Players take turns calling out ordered pairs to guess the location of their opponent's ships. If there is no ship at that plot point, the opponent says *miss*, and the player marks that point with an *X* on the grid labeled *My Opponent's Grid*. If there is a ship, the opponent says *hit*, and the player circles that point. When players think they have sunk one of their opponent's ships, they write the ordered pairs of the ship's coordinates. The winner is the first player to sink all of his or her partner's ships.

7. At the conclusion of the game, have students trade coordinate grids to verify that they wrote the ordered pairs correctly.

Extended Learning

For higher-level math learning, invite students to use coordinate grids with four quadrants, so they are working with both positive and negative numbers.

978-1-4129-5929-2

Sink It! Game Grids

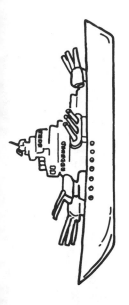

Directions: Use the first grid to mark coordinate points for your ships.
Use the second grid to mark hits and misses for your opponent's ships.

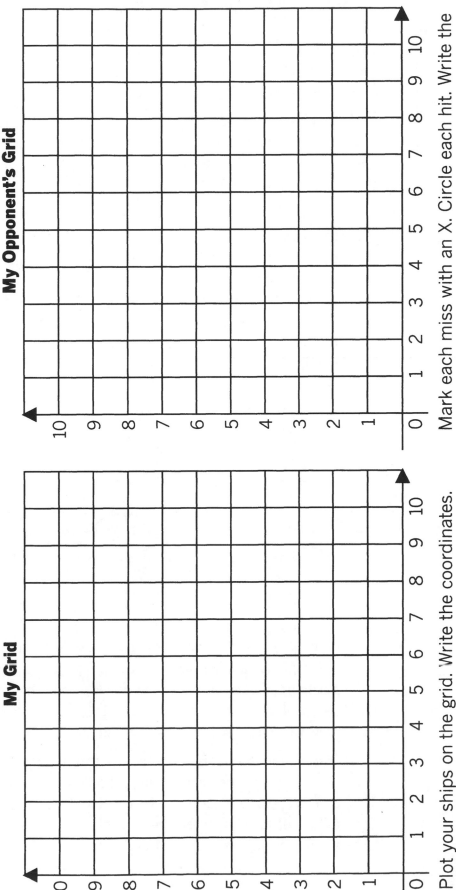

My Grid

10
9
8
7
6
5
4
3
2
1

0 1 2 3 4 5 6 7 8 9 10

Plot your ships on the grid. Write the coordinates.
Tugboat: (__,__)
Sailboat: (__,__) (__,__)
Yacht: (__,__) (__,__) (__,__)
Submarine: (__,__) (__,__) (__,__) (__,__)
Destroyer: (__,__) (__,__) (__,__) (__,__) (__,__)

My Opponent's Grid

10
9
8
7
6
5
4
3
2
1

0 1 2 3 4 5 6 7 8 9 10

Mark each miss with an X. Circle each hit. Write the
coordinates of your opponent's ships.
Tugboat: (__,__)
Sailboat: (__,__) (__,__)
Yacht: (__,__) (__,__) (__,__)
Submarine: (__,__) (__,__) (__,__) (__,__)
Destroyer: (__,__) (__,__) (__,__) (__,__) (__,__)

Probability Portrait

Materials
- Probability Portrait reproducible
- paper plates
- markers or crayons
- large paper clips
- pencils
- coins

Objective
Students will predict the probability of a coin landing heads up or tails up and then conduct an experiment to test their predictions.

Estimating "the odds" of something happening, otherwise known as *probability*, is an important math skill. This game gives students the opportunity to predict outcomes and then experiment to determine the probability of a coin landing heads up or tails up.

1. Prepare six paper-plate spinners. Divide each plate into equal sections to represent halves, thirds, fourths, fifths, sixths, and eighths. Then use different colors of crayons or markers to color in the sections of each circle to represent different outcomes for probability experiments. For example: Halves—Color one section blue and the other section red so the probability of landing on blue is one in two, or 1/2. Each plate can represent the outcome of your choice.

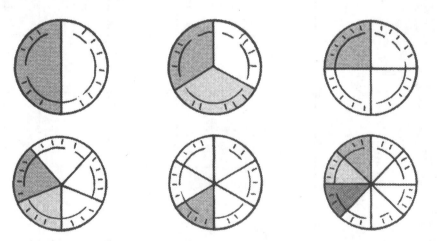

2. Divide the class into six small groups. Give each group one paper-plate spinner, a large paper clip, and a pencil. Demonstrate how to position the point of the pencil in one end of the paper clip at the center of the paper plate, and spin the paper clip. Tell students that they will use these spinners to conduct probability experiments.

3. Discuss the math terms *probability* and *outcome*. Explain that each group will determine the probability of the spinner landing on each color and write it as a fraction. Model the process. After they have recorded the possible outcomes, have students experiment with the spinner and keep a tally of the results. Then have groups trade spinners and repeat a new set of experiments.

4. After completing the first set of probability experiments, divide the class into pairs and give each student a copy of the **Probability Portrait reproducible (page 46)**. Explain that they will play a probability game. Give each pair of students a coin. Ask: *What is the probability of the coin landing either heads up or tails up?* (one in two tosses, or 1/2)

5. Demonstrate how to play the game. First, each player must estimate how many times they think the coin will land heads up and tails up. Player 1 tosses the coin. If the coin lands heads up, the player colors in one square on his or her Probability Portrait using one color. If it lands tails up, the player colors the square using a different color. Then it is Player 2's turn to toss the coin.

6. Players take turns tossing the coin and coloring in each square with the corresponding color to tally the results. When all the squares of the portrait are filled in, players will have each tossed the coin 100 times. Players then count the number of squares for each color and write this number at the bottom of the reproducible. The player whose estimate was closest to the actual number wins the game.

7. After students finish playing the game, discuss the results. Ask them to explain why the coin didn't land heads up or tails up in equal numbers, even though the possible outcome was one out of every two tosses.

Probability Portrait

Directions: Write your estimates at the bottom of the page. Then toss the coin 100 times. Color the squares a different color for heads and tails. Then record your results.

	Estimate	Actual
Heads Up		
Tails Up		

CHAPTER 3

Science

What Am I?

Objective
Students will review the interdependence of plants and animals within different ecosystems.

Learning about the populations and habitats that exist within an ecosystem helps students better understand the complex world in which they live. In this guessing game, students will review the plants and animals that live in various ecosystems.

Materials
- reference materials about ecosystems
- butcher paper
- art supplies
- index cards
- tape

1. Divide the class into small groups. Provide reference materials such as textbooks, encyclopedias, and Internet articles for each group to research one specific ecosystem. Give each group a sheet of butcher paper and instruct them to make a poster describing the plants and animals visitors might find in that region.

2. Mount travel posters on the wall and allow time for each group to share information from their poster. Then distribute an index card to each student. Direct students to choose one plant or animal from their group's ecosystem and write its name on the card. Collect the cards.

3. Tell students that they will play a game to review plants and animals found in various ecosystems. Tape one card to each student's back. Then invite students to circulate around the room asking each other *yes* or *no* questions about who they might be. Model a few appropriate questions, such as: *Am I a mammal? Do I like to swim? Am I a carnivore?*

4. Play continues until all the animals are guessed. After the game, invite volunteers to share what life would be like as a plant or animal living in a particular ecosystem.

Food-Chain Tag

Materials
• video or book about ecosystems
• construction paper
• yarn

Objective
Students will learn about the relationship between producers and consumers in an ecosystem.

Fourth graders learn about animals and plants in a variety of ecosystems. This game will help them better understand the relationship between producers and consumers and ways in which these interactions can affect the food chain.

1. Watch a documentary video or read a nonfiction picture book to review an ecosystem such as a prairie. When finished, discuss terms such as *producer, consumer, food chain,* and *food web.* Ask students to name different plants and animals found in the ecosystem (e.g., *grass, flowers, grasshoppers, mice, squirrels, prairie dogs, snakes, bison, hawks*). Classify each one as a plant, carnivore, herbivore, or omnivore.

2. Invite students to list on the board different food chains in the ecosystem. For example: *seeds–mice–snakes–hawks.*

3. Tell students that they will play a game of tag that demonstrates the relationship between producers and consumers in an ecosystem. Choose one student to be a hawk. Choose two students to be snakes. Choose eight students to be mice. To help identify these animals, distribute nametag necklaces made of construction paper and yarn. Have students write the name of their animal on their nametag. The remaining students are seeds and do not need nametags.

4. Take students outdoors, and then explain the rules: *The hawk can only tag snakes. Snakes can only tag mice. Mice can only tag seeds. Seeds don't tag anyone but try to run away. Anyone who is tagged sits down immediately and is out of the game.*

5. Play a sample round of tag to check that students understand the rules. Remind them of some general tag rules, such as only tagging appropriate parts of the body and using a gentle tap rather than a forceful tag. The game is over when no one can tag anyone else. Count the number of animals and seeds left in the game. Identify which animals are out. Discuss the results.

6. Switch nametags to get one new hawk, two new snakes, and eight new mice. Play the game again. When you're finished, discuss the new results. Play the game several times, switching nametags each time. Compare the results from each game.

7. When you're finished playing, talk about what might happen to disrupt a real ecosystem, for example: *Hunters might kill all the snakes, and there wouldn't be enough food for the hawk to catch. In addition, there would be too many mice left, and they would eat all the seeds.*

Extended Learning

Discuss how natural disasters, pollution, or human interference might upset the balance of a food chain in an ecosystem. Invite students to research one natural disaster, source of pollution, or human interference in an ecosystem. Ask them to share their findings with the class and brainstorm some possible solutions to the problems.

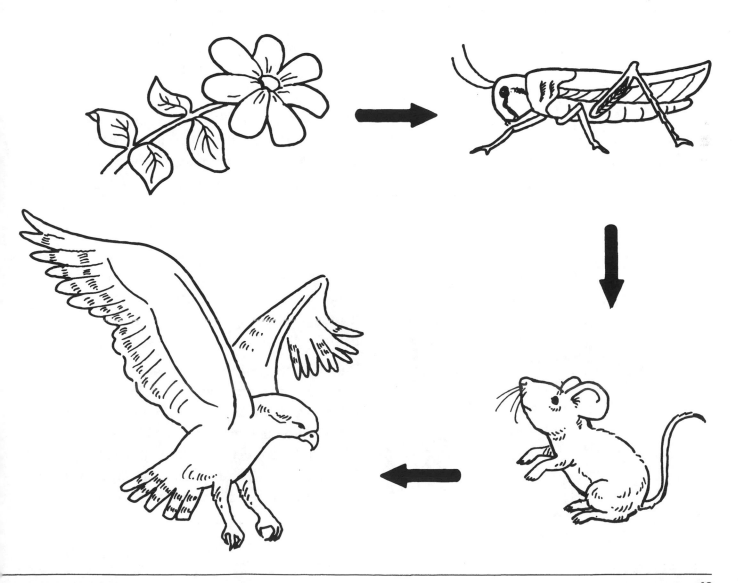

"Our Changing Earth" Game Show

Materials
- "Our Changing Earth" Game Cards reproducibles
- reference materials about natural disasters
- pocket chart
- index cards
- cardstock
- scissors
- timer

Objective
Students will review physical features of the earth's surface and how they change.

The news is filled with information about our changing world. Earthquakes shake and reshape mountains. Volcanoes erupt. Heavy rains cause mudslides. As students study the physical features of the earth and how they change over time, this game will help them review what they have learned.

1. Ask students to act as news reporters and gather information about recent natural disasters caused by geological changes, such as earthquakes, tsunamis, volcanic eruptions, and mudslides. Allow time for students to collect information during class from the Internet or newspapers, or assign this as homework. Invite them to share what they have learned with the class.

2. Set up the game by making five columns in a pocket chart. Use index cards to label the five columns (e.g., *Water, Mountains, Volcanoes, Earthquakes, Continents.*) and point values (e.g., *10, 20, 30, 40, 50*).

3. Copy a set of the **"Our Changing Earth" Game Cards reproducibles (pages 52–54)** on cardstock. Cut out the cards and sort them by category. Place one question card behind each point card in the pocket chart. (You may use the question cards provided, or make your own.) Hide the *DOUBLE POINTS!* card behind one of the questions. If a team answers this question correctly, they earn double points.

4. Tell students they will play a game to help them review facts about the earth's surface and how it changes. Divide the class into several small teams. Ask each team to choose a team name.

5. Demonstrate how to play the game. A player from the first team asks for a column and a point value (e.g., *Mountains for 30*). After you read aloud the question behind that card (taking care to conceal the answer from students), set the timer for one minute. Let the player quietly confer with teammates to select an answer. The student must answer before time is up.

WATER
Q: What percentage of the earth is covered by water?
A: About 70%

MOUNTAINS
Q: Which has more height, hills or mountains?
A: Mountains

VOLCANOES
Q: Which state is made of volcanic islands?
A: Hawaii

6. If the player guesses incorrectly, the first player on the second team has a chance to answer. Each team gets a turn until the correct answer is given. The team that answers correctly scores the points. Before starting the game, make sure students understand the rules and point system.

7. It is now the second team's turn to choose a column and a point value (e.g., *Volcanoes for 50*). Play continues around the room, going from team to team and progressing from player to player, so everyone has a chance to participate. The team with the most points at the end wins the game.

8. After the game, allow students to reflect in their journals on what they learned about the earth's physical features. Ask them to write one new thing they learned about the feature or change (volcanoes, mountains, earthquakes, continents, water) that interests them the most.

"OUR CHANGING EARTH" GAME SHOW

Water	Mountains	Volcanoes	Earthquakes	Continents
10	10	10	10	10
20	20	20	20	20
30	30	30	30	30
40	40	40	40	40
50	50	50	50	50

"Our Changing Earth" Game Cards

CONTINENTS
Q: Which theory states that the earth's continents are constantly moving?

A: *Continental drift*

CONTINENTS
Q: The two main features of Earth are continents and what?

A: *Oceans*

CONTINENTS
Q: Which of these three earth layers make up the land we know as continents: core, mantle, or crust?

A: *Crust*

CONTINENTS
Q: Name at least five continents.

A: *Africa, Antarctica, Asia, Australia, Europe, North America, South America*

CONTINENTS
Q: On which continent do we find the United States?

A: *North America*

CONTINENTS
Q: Which of the seven continents is the world's largest island and smallest continent?

A: *Australia*

VOLCANOES
Q: Which state is made up of volcanic islands?

A: *Hawaii*

VOLCANOES
Q: What is magma, or molten rock, that reaches the surface of the earth?

A: *Lava*

VOLCANOES
Q: What is the name for the many volcanoes located around the Pacific Ocean?

A: *The Ring of Fire*

DOUBLE POINTS!

"Our Changing Earth" Game Cards

VOLCANOES
Q: What is the opening at the mouth of a volcano called?

A: *Crater*

VOLCANOES
Q: What shape do most volcanoes form?

A: *Cone*

VOLCANOES
Q: What do you call a volcano that is sleeping but may still erupt sometime in the future?

A: *Dormant*

EARTHQUAKES
Q: What is a crack in the earth's crust called?

A: *Fault*

EARTHQUAKES
Q: What instrument is used to measure seismic waves?

A: *Seismograph*

EARTHQUAKES
Q: (True or False) Many earthquakes take place near the edges of continental plates.

A: *True*

EARTHQUAKES
Q: What is the center of an earthquake called?

A: *Epicenter*

EARTHQUAKES
Q: What scale is used to measure the strength of an earthquake?

A: *Richter scale*

EARTHQUAKES
Q: What are smaller earthquakes that occur after the main shock called?

A: *Aftershocks*

WATER
Q: What percentage of the earth is covered by water?

A: *About 70%*

"Our Changing Earth" Game Cards

WATER

Q: What huge canyon was carved out by the Colorado River?

A: *The Grand Canyon*

WATER

Q: What is new land formed at a river's mouth from deposits carried downstream?

A: *Delta*

WATER

Q: What is it called when water wears away soil and carries it away?

A: *Erosion*

WATER

Q: What large body of ice moves slowly down a mountain, eroding soil and forming a huge valley?

A: *Glacier*

WATER

Q: What large bodies of salt water deposit sand on the shores to make beaches?

A: *Oceans*

MOUNTAINS

Q: What is the earth's highest mountain range?

A: *The Himalayas*

MOUNTAINS

Q: (True or False) Many mountains are formed where continental plates collide.

A: *True*

MOUNTAINS

Q: What is the name of the earth's longest mountain range, found underneath the ocean?

A: *Mid-Atlantic Range*

MOUNTAINS

Q: Which has more height, hills or mountains?

A: *Mountains*

MOUNTAINS

Q: What is the highest mountain peak in the world?

A: *Mount Everest*

Rock Rummy

Objective
Students will review properties and common uses of minerals and rocks.

From sparkling gems to ordinary gravel, rocks and minerals are everywhere. While students enjoy investigating different minerals, they may also be surprised to discover the many ways people use these materials. In this game, students will learn and review the classification, properties, and common uses of nearly 20 minerals and rocks.

Materials
- Rock Rummy Game Cards reproducibles
- cardstock
- scissors
- magnifying glasses
- penny
- index cards

1. Prepare for the game by making three sets of matching game cards. Reproduce the **Rock Rummy Game Cards reproducibles (pages 57–58)** on cardstock for a total of 60 cards. Cut out the cards, and laminate them for durability if you wish.

2. Introduce the game by taking students on a short walk around the school grounds and having each student collect one rock. Back in the classroom, divide the class into small groups. Give each group a magnifying glass and each student an index card. Invite students to examine their rocks with a magnifying glass and write their observations on their index cards. They may describe properties such as size, shape, weight, color, and texture.

3. Demonstrate how to test a rock for hardness by trying to scratch it first with a fingernail, then with a penny, and finally with another student's rock. Have students record observations on their index cards. Provide time for students to investigate each other's rocks.

4. Discuss what students learned while observing the rocks. Point out the fact that various rocks have different degrees of hardness and this hardness can be measured. Introduce or review the Mohs Scale of Hardness (page 56).

5. Discuss terms such as *mineral* and *rock*. Talk about the three types of rock (e.g., *igneous, sedimentary, metamorphic*) and how each is formed. If possible, let students examine common products made from minerals and rocks (e.g., baby talc from mineral talc, floor tile from sedimentary rock sandstone, pedicare stick from igneous rock pumice).

6. Tell students they will play a rummy card game to review the classification, properties, and common uses of minerals and rocks. A group of two to four students may play at a time. Demonstrate how to play the game before students play independently.

7. Mix up all 60 cards. Deal eight cards to each player. Place the remaining cards facedown in a pile. Turn over the top card and place it faceup in a separate stack to start the discard pile.

8. During a turn, players may lay down sets of three cards at a time. The goal is to make sets of three matching cards. This may include a set of any three rocks of the same type (e.g., igneous rocks, sedimentary rocks, or metamorphic rocks), or a set of three minerals in a row according to their numerical value on the hardness scale (e.g., 4, 5, 6 or 6, 7, 8). A wild card may be used to complete any set. When their turn is over, players discard one card from their hand faceup on the discard pile.

9. The dealer goes first and may either take the top card from the discard pile or a card from the stack. If the player can make a set of three cards, he or she places them faceup on the table. When no more sets can be made, the player discards and the next player gets a turn. The first player to lay down all of his or her cards in sets of three wins the game.

10. After the game, provide time for students to write in their journals about what they learned.

Mohs Scale of Hardness

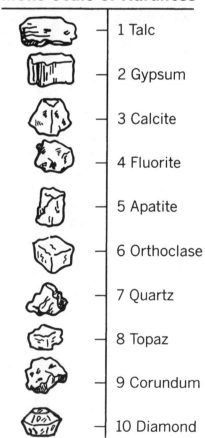

1 Talc

2 Gypsum

3 Calcite

4 Fluorite

5 Apatite

6 Orthoclase

7 Quartz

8 Topaz

9 Corundum

10 Diamond

Rock Rummy Game Cards

✂

6 Hardness Scale		1 Hardness Scale
6 Orthoclase		1 Talc
Common Use: Porcelain Sinks		Common Use: Baby Powder
Mineral		Mineral

7 Hardness Scale		2 Hardness Scale
7 Quartz		2 Gypsum
Common Use: Optical Lenses		Common Use: Plaster
Mineral		Mineral

8 Hardness Scale		3 Hardness Scale
8 Topaz		3 Calcite
Common Use: Jewelry		Common Use: Cement
Mineral		Mineral

9 Hardness Scale		4 Hardness Scale
9 Corundum		4 Flourite
Common Use: Jewelry		Common Use: Mineral Collections
Mineral		Mineral

10 Hardness Scale		5 Hardness Scale
10 Diamond		5 Apatite
Common Use: Jewelry		Common Use: Fertilizer
Mineral		Mineral

Rock Rummy Game Cards

Sedimentary / Chert	Common Use: Ancient Arrowheads	**Rock**
	WILD CARD!	
Sedimentary / Limestone	Common Use: Buildings	**Rock**
Metamorphic / Coal	Common Use: Produce Electricity	**Rock**
Igneous / Pumice	Common Use: Foot Care	**Rock**
Metamorphic / Marble	Common Use: Statues	**Rock**
Igneous / Granite	Common Use: Countertops	**Rock**
Metamorphic / Slate	Common Use: Chalkboards	**Rock**
Igneous / Obsidian	Common Use: Ancient Spearheads	**Rock**
Sedimentary / Sandstone	Common Use: Tile Floors	**Rock**

Reproducible

978-1-4129-5929-2 • © Corwin Press

Go North!

Objective

Students will use a compass to move in different directions on a game board.

Locating directions is a skill that students will use throughout their lives. In this game, students practice locating north, south, east, and west within the classroom.

Materials
- paper plates (or tagboard circles)
- large paper clips
- brass brads
- chart paper
- compasses
- construction paper (or floor mat from Twister® game)
- masking tape
- map of city or state

1. To prepare for the game, use a paper plate (or tagboard circle), brad, and paper clip to create a spinner for each group. Divide the plate into four equal sections labeled *Go North, Go East, Go West,* and *Go South*. Poke a brad through the center of the plate and attach a paper clip as the spinner.

2. Explain to students that magnets serve an important purpose: *Because the earth is like a huge magnet, the needle in a magnetic compass points north. People use a compass to help them find directions.* Demonstrate how an actual compass works. Work together and use the compass to locate north, south, east, and west in your classroom. Post a chart-paper sign on each wall indicating the direction.

3. Show students a map of your state. Explain that maps are made using a compass. Point out the compass rose on the map and identify north, south, east, and west. Ask students to identify landmarks north of your classroom on the map. Then ask them to point in the direction of these landmarks. Students should point to the sign you posted on the north wall. Repeat this activity for landmarks south, east, and west of your classroom.

4. Tell students that they will use a compass to determine which way to move on a game board. Choose a group of two to eight students to play the first game. Give them a real compass, a photocopy of the Go North! compass (page 60), a spinner, and a floor mat from a Twister® (a registered trademark of Hasbro, Inc.) game (or make your own from construction paper circles taped to the floor in a 4 x 6 grid pattern).

5. Position the mat on the floor so the top row of four circles is facing north. Place the Go North! compass on the floor nearby so *north* is pointing in the correct direction. Use the real compass to check the position of both the mat and the Go North! compass.

6. Show students how to play the game. For the first game, you can spin the spinner. Players each step on the mat and stand on one circle of their choice. No two players can start on the same circle.

7. Spin the spinner, and call out the direction. Each player must move off the original circle and take one step in that direction to stand on a new circle. Check that students move in the correct direction. Continue playing, spinning the spinner for each new turn and moving as indicated. If at any time a player runs out of room and is forced to step off the mat, he or she is out of the game. The last player remaining on the mat wins the game. The winner becomes the spinner for the next game.

8. After everyone has a turn, ask students to share how people determine directions in their daily lives (e.g., *use a map, use a compass, look up directions on the Internet*).

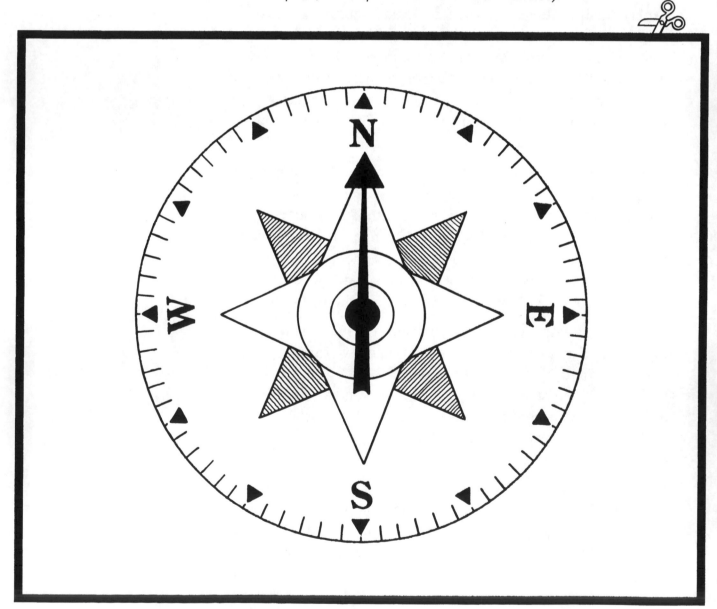

Electric Circuit Match Game

Objective

Students will construct electrical circuits and test their work with a circuit tester.

Electricity is one scientific concept that is easily observable. Students can watch how an electric current flows along a circuit and discover how an electric current passes easily through conductors, but not through insulators. For this game, students will match questions with the correct answers by using a circuit tester.

1. To prepare for the game, make a tester for each pair of students. Begin by folding a sheet of construction paper in half to resemble a file folder. Use the hole punch to punch a column of four holes through both layers of paper along the fold. Punch a second column of four holes along the open edge opposite the fold.

2. Tear off an 8" x 12" sheet of foil and fold it over itself four times to form a 1/2" x 12" strip. Make four foil strips per student. Then make circuit testers by looping one end of a 1 1/2-foot length of wire securely around the base of a lightbulb. Tape the other end of the wire securely to the negative end of a battery.

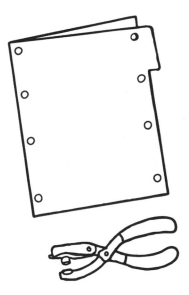

3. Show various samples of conductors to students, such as bare electrical wire, screws, and aluminum foil. Tell students: *Most metals are good conductors, materials through which an electric current can easily pass.*

4. Then show students various samples of insulators, such as a plastic spoon, wooden craft stick, and masking tape. Tell them: *Many materials are insulators, materials through which an electric current cannot easily pass.*

5. Show an example of a circuit that uses one battery, a miniature lightbulb, an electrical wire, and a strip of aluminum foil. Move one end of the electrical wire on and off the foil strip to demonstrate how an electric current moves along a path called a *circuit*. Ask students to point out the conductors and the insulators in your

sample circuit. *(Plastic insulation on wire is an insulator, and metal wire or metal parts of a lightbulb are conductors.)*

6. Give each student a construction-paper folder. Demonstrate how to position the folder so it opens like a book with the fold at the left. Instruct each student to write four questions and corresponding answers on a separate piece of scrap paper. Questions can relate to electricity, another area of the science curriculum you are studying, or any topic of your choice. Check students' questions and answers.

What is a series circuit?   Metal

What is a parallel circuit?   A circuit with more than one path

What is a good conductor?   Masking tape

What is an insulator?   A circuit with one path

7. On the outside of the folder, have students write their four questions along the left column of holes, one question beside each hole. Tell them to mix up their answers in a different order and write them along the right column of holes, one answer beside each hole.

8. Distribute four foil strips and two 2-foot lengths of masking tape to each student. Show students how to connect the first question to the correct answer by placing a foil strip over both corresponding holes. Be sure both holes are completely covered by the foil. Demonstrate how to insulate the circuit by covering the entire foil strip with masking tape. Continue to connect the remaining three questions and answers down the folder. Close the folder so the foil strips are inside and the questions are on top.

9. Have students check their own work with the circuit testers. Tell them to press the positive end of the battery on the foil in the hole next to the first question. Simultaneously, press the base of the lightbulb on the foil in the hole next to the correct answer. If the bulb lights up, the correct answer was chosen and the circuit was successfully completed. (If foil strips are not insulated correctly, more than one answer will light the bulb.) Have students check that their folder games operate correctly. Add more tape as needed to better insulate foil circuits.

10. Use a volunteer's file game (or one you created) to demonstrate how to play. Press the battery on the foil in the hole next to the first question. Read the question aloud. Then read all four answers aloud, guessing which one is correct. Press the base of the lightbulb on the foil in the hole next to your chosen answer. If the bulb lights up, the answer is correct. Repeat this process with the other three questions until you find all the correct answers.

11. Provide time for students to pair up and play their partners' games. Afterwards, ask students to discuss what they learned about electric currents, circuits, conductors, and insulators.

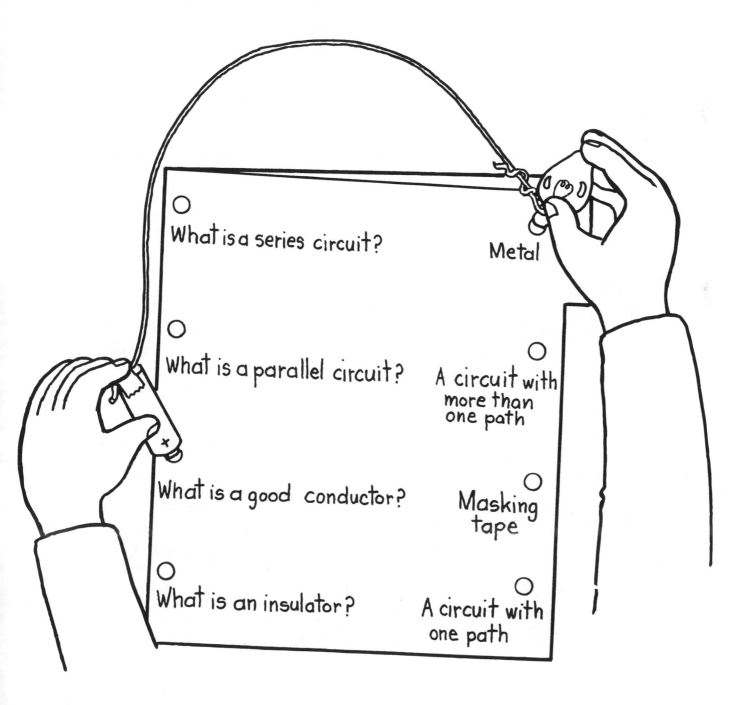

CHAPTER 4

Social Studies

Footprints Through History

Objective

Students will review content about the history of their state.

Materials
- references about your state
- construction paper
- scissors
- markers
- masking tape
- coin

This game provides an engaging review of your state's people, places, and cultural heritage. In this kinesthetic game, student groups play on a giant game board in which they become the markers moving from space to space while answering review questions.

1. Remind students of some of the topics recently discussed in your study of state history. Ask each student to write an ending to the following sentence: *If I had a time machine that sent me back in time in our state, I would want to meet (or see) _____.* Have students discuss their answers with a partner.

2. Divide the class into small groups of three or four students. Assign each group a different topic to review, such as natural regions, early peoples, statehood, or modern economy.

3. Provide each group with references containing information about your state, such as textbooks, encyclopedias, or access to the Internet. Ask each group to write a numbered list of ten questions and answers relating to their assigned topic. When finished, check their work for accuracy and spelling. Have each group write a final copy of the ten numbered questions and answers. This is the answer key.

4. Provide students with construction paper, scissors, and markers. Have them trace and cut out a total of 20 footprints. (For a longer game, create 30 or 40 footprints.) Then ask them to number ten of the footprints *1–10*. On two of the remaining footprints, write *START,* and on two more write *FINISH.* Use the remaining six footprints to write the following commands, one per print: *Go Ahead 1, Go Ahead 2, Go Ahead 3, Go Back 1, Skip Next Turn,* and *Take Another Turn.*

5. Then help students make a giant game board on your classroom floor or another open area. Help them lay out the board by placing the two *START* footprints side-by-side on the ground so a student can stand on them. Place the rest of the footprints on the

ground in order from *1–10,* moving away from *START.* Randomly add in the extra footprints along the path. Place the two *FINISH* footprints at the end of the game board. After footprints are in position, tape them to the ground.

6. Then explain to student how to play the game:
   a. One group can play at a time. First, the group chooses one volunteer to be the "Keeper of the Key" (answer key). This student holds the answer key and a coin, and does not play the game.
   b. The first player stands with both feet on *START.* The Keeper of the Key gives the coin to the first player, who tosses it in the air. Heads indicates that the player moves forward one space; tails indicates two spaces. The first player moves forward accordingly, stands on the footprint, and follows the instructions. (If multiple students land on the same footprint, they stand together in a row.)
   c. If the player lands on a numbered footprint, the Keeper of the Key asks that player the corresponding question. (If a different player lands on that same footprint later in the game, the Keeper asks the same question. Repeated questions and answers reinforce learning.) If the player guesses incorrectly, the Keeper reads the correct answer from the Key. Whether the answer is correct or incorrect, the player remains on that space.
   d. It is now the second player's turn. Play continues until one player reaches the *FINISH* footprints. The winner becomes the Keeper of the Key in the next game.

7. After every group has a chance to play, they can switch questions with other groups and play again. When finished, allow time for students to write in their journals about some of the things they learned about their state.

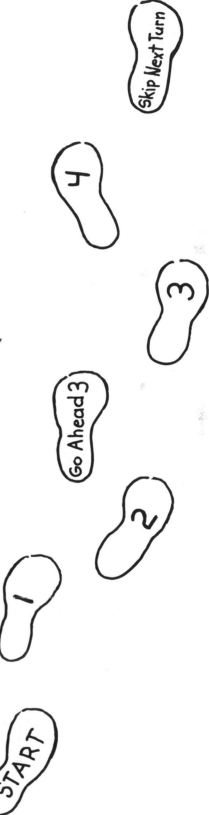

Our State Government

Objective
Students will review the executive branch, legislative branch, and judicial branch of their state government.

Many students are already familiar with some of the current leaders of their state's government. After you have taught about the different branches of state government and your state's elected officials, use this game to help students review what they have learned.

Materials
- State Government Game Board reproducible
- State Government Game Cards reproducible
- scissors
- state map
- pictures of your state's capitol, current governor, members of your state legislature, and state supreme court justices (most are available on the Internet)
- dice

1. Review aspects of your state government with students. Use a state map to show the location of the capital city. Show students a picture of your state capitol and some of your current elected officials, including your governor and several members of your state's legislative and judicial branches.

2. Tell students: *The legislative branch establishes the laws. The executive branch executes the laws. The judicial branch makes sure the laws are obeyed.* Discuss how the state constitution lists the laws that govern the state, and how the state budget provides finances to serve the state's residents.

3. Tell students they will play a game to review your state's government. Divide the class into small groups of two to four players. Give each player a copy of the **State Government Game Board reproducible (page 68)** and a set of cards cut from the **State Government Game Cards reproducible (page 69)**. Have students fill in the name of your state, the capital city, and your governor on the game board.

4. Demonstrate how to play the game. Give each group one die, and ask players to mix up their cards and place them facedown in a pile on the table.
   a. The first player rolls the die and draws no more than three cards from the stack until he or she draws a match. For example, if the player rolls a 1, for *State Capitol*, he or she draws cards until finding a fact about the state capitol. If the player does not find a matching card in three draws, he or she must forfeit the turn. The player then places the cards on the bottom of the deck.
   b. If the player does find a matching card, he or she places the card on the game board in the corresponding square. Then it's the next player's turn.

c. Play continues clockwise around the group. Check that players are placing the cards in the correct boxes on the reproducible. Act as the "judge" to solve any disagreements between players.

d. As play continues, players might roll the number of a topic they have already completed on their game board. If this happens, that player must skip his or her turn. The first player to correctly place all 18 cards on his or her game board wins the game.

5. After the game, ask students to share which part of the state government they think is most important and why. Invite them to share ideas about what they might like to change or how they could contribute.

Answer Key

State Capitol: Where members of the state legislature meet to make new laws; Located in the state's capital city; Where the governor gives the State of the State Address each year.

Legislative Branch: Establishes state laws; Made up of two parts—the Senate and the Assembly; Votes on ways to spend the state budget.

Executive Branch: Executes state laws; Governor is the main leader; Leaders are appointed by the governor or voted into office.

Judicial Branch: Makes sure state laws are obeyed; Decides whether laws are fair; Made up of judges appointed by the governor.

State Constitution: Lists the laws that govern the state; Describes how the state government is run; Lists the rights and freedoms of state citizens.

State Budget: Provides the finances to serve the state's residents; Uses taxes collected from state citizens; Pays for road improvements and public education.

Extended Learning

Divide the class into small groups and assign each group one of the topics from the game—*State Capitol, State Budget, State Legislative Branch, State Judicial Branch, State Executive Branch,* and *State Constitution.* Instruct each group to work together to make a poster on butcher paper, showing different ways these things or people contribute to the state and help keep it going.

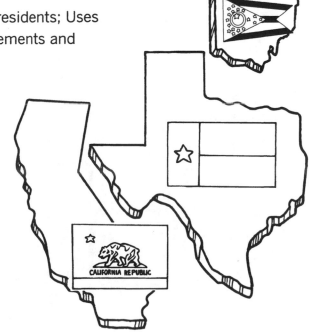

State Government Game Board

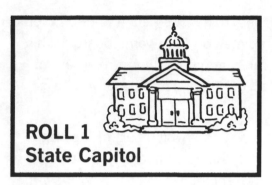

ROLL 1
State Capitol

State:

_____

Capital City:

_____

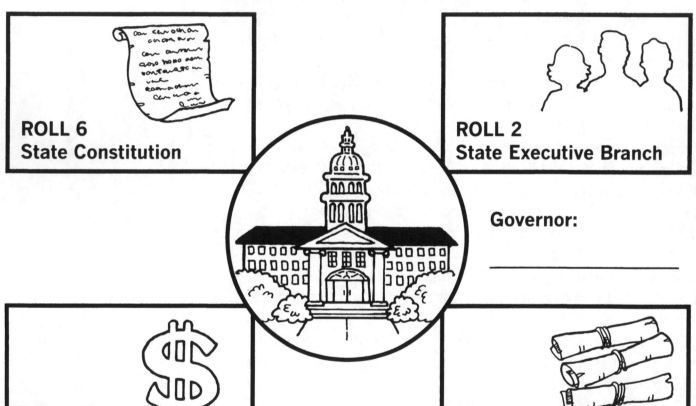

ROLL 6
State Constitution

ROLL 2
State Executive Branch

Governor:

_____

ROLL 5
State Budget

ROLL 3
State Legislative Branch

ROLL 4
State Judicial Branch

State Government Game Cards

Where members of the state legislature meet to make new laws	Located in the state's capital city	Where the governor gives the State of the State Address each year
Establishes state laws	Made up of two parts—the Senate and the Assembly	Votes on ways to spend the state budget
Executes state laws	Governor is the main leader	Leaders are appointed by the governor or voted into office
Makes sure state laws are obeyed	Decides whether laws are fair	Made up of judges appointed by the governor
Lists the laws that govern the state	Describes how the state government is run	Lists the rights and freedoms of state citizens
Provides the finances to serve the state's residents	Uses taxes collected from state citizens	Pays for road improvements and public education

Geography Bingo

Materials

- Geography Bingo Card reproducible
- photographs of local natural attractions
- construction paper
- scissors
- references about geography
- butcher paper
- art supplies

Objective

Students will learn about the natural regions of their state and the physical features in each region.

Every state contains distinct natural regions. After students learn about the unique physical features in each region of their state, they can review what they've learned with an exciting game of Bingo.

1. Select four or five photographs of important natural attractions in your state. Display the photographs and ask students to guess where each one was taken. Write each guess on the board before revealing the answer.

2. Assign each student one of the photos to research, using encyclopedias, social studies books, or Internet resources. Ask students to write one fact about the natural feature, and then meet in small groups to compile facts about each natural feature. Have each group share its findings with the class.

3. Explain to students that they will play a Bingo game to review natural regions in your state and the physical features in each region. On the board, write a list of five natural regions in your state (e.g., *coast, plains, mountains, valley, desert*). If your state does not have five distinct regions, include major bodies of water as well.

4. Invite students to brainstorm and list physical features found in each region. Some features will be listed in more than one region (e.g., *lake*). Add major cities, landmarks, animals, and plants found in each region until you have exactly 15 items listed for each region. (If you plan to play the game numerous times, copy the list you brainstormed onto a piece of paper to use in future games.)

5. Give each student a copy of the **Geography Bingo Card reproducible (page 72)** and a piece of construction paper. Instruct students to write five regions across the top of the Bingo card and fill in the columns with five items that can be found in each region. Check that they only write items from the list on the board. Have students cut the construction paper into one-inch squares to use as game markers.

978-1-4129-5929-2

6. Demonstrate how to play the game by calling out a region and something found in that region, such as: *Mountains—waterfall*. Students should then check their Bingo cards. If they wrote *waterfall* in the column for *Mountains*, they cover that space with a paper marker. (They do *not* cover the space if they wrote *waterfall* in the column for a different region, such as *Valley*.) Check off that item from the list on the board. Tell students you will continue calling out regions and items found in those regions until someone covers five spaces vertically, horizontally, or diagonally on their game card.

7. Then continue the game by calling out and checking off a second region and one item found there, such as: *Valley—river*. Students cover that space with a marker if they wrote it on their game card. Continue playing the game until one player covers five markers in a row, vertically, horizontally, or diagonally, and calls out: *Bingo!*

8. After the game, invite student groups to use butcher paper and art supplies to create a mural for each region discussed. Encourage them to add various plants and animals found in that region, and label each item.

Variation of the Game

Alter the game by having students cover all four corners, only one region (one column, such as *Mountains*), or all 25 squares of the game card before calling: *Bingo!*

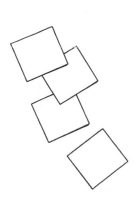

Name _____ Date _____

Geography Bingo Card

B	I	N	G	O
Region	Region	Region	Region	Region
Northern Coast	Southern Coast	Mountains	Valley	Desert
coastal ranges	coastal plain	volcano	waterfalls	plateau
ocean	islands	Sierra Nevadas	Yosemite Valley	basin
San Andreas Fault	ocean	FREE SPACE	bears	Mojave Desert
whales	San Andreas Fault	waterfalls	San Joaquin	cacti
cliffs	Los Angeles	Mount Whitney	farms	cactus wrens

Name _____ Date _____

Geography Bingo Card

B	I	N	G	O
Region	Region	Region	Region	Region
		FREE SPACE		

Alphabet Hunt

Objective

Students will review the natural resources and industries in their state.

As students learn more about the state they call home, they discover that natural resources provide the materials needed for industries to thrive. In this game, students will review your state's natural resources and main industries.

1. To review what students have learned about your state's natural resources, ask volunteers to help you list on the board specific natural resources found in your state (e.g., *soil, water, natural fuel, minerals, animals*). Make a second list of main industries that thrive in your state (e.g., *farming, steel industry, oil production*).

2. Teach students the following song, sung to the tune of "The Farmer in the Dell."

Our State Is Great!

Our resources are great.
Our resources are great.
Heigh, ho, the derry-o
Our resources are great.

Our state has lots of _____.
Our state has lots of _____.
Heigh, ho, the derry-o
Our state has lots of _____.

Our industries are great.
Our industries are great.
Heigh, ho, the derry-o
Our industries are great.

Our state makes lots of _____.
Our state makes lots of _____.
Heigh, ho, the derry-o
Our state makes lots of _____.

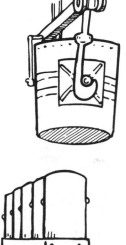

3. Ask a student to choose one natural resource and one industry in your state (e.g., *apples, steel*). Then sing the song together, plugging those words into the blanks. Ask volunteers to suggest additional verses.

4. When finished, explain to students that they will play a game to review the natural resources and industries found in your state. Give each student a copy of the **Alphabet Hunt Game Board reproducible (page 75)**.

5. Divide the class into small groups of three or four players. Then work with one group to model how to play the game. The first player chooses one letter of the alphabet. The other players then cross that letter off the list at the top of their game board. Players then quickly write five words starting with that letter to fit each category. For example: *S—strawberries, squash, sheep, soil, steel.* All players stop writing when the first player announces: *I'm done!*

6. Check that players have written natural resources and industries in the correct categories. Each player then totals his or her score for that round, using the point system on the game board.

Our state has lots of apples!

7. Invite students to play on their own, while you circulate around the room, providing assistance as needed. As students play, check that they are writing words in the correct categories. Have groups continue playing for ten rounds, with a different player choosing a new letter for each round. The winner is the player who scores the most points.

8. After the game, ask students which of their state industries and natural resources can be found in the same community in which they live.

Name _____ Date _____

Alphabet Hunt Game Board

A B C D E F G H I J K L M N O P Q R S T U V W X Y Z

	Fruit 2 points (1 point if someone else has the same answer.)	Vegetable 2 points (1 point if someone else has the same answer.)	Animal 2 points (1 point if someone else has the same answer.)	Natural Resource 10 points (5 points if someone else has the same answer.)	Industry 10 points (5 points if someone else has the same answer.)	Points
1.						
2.						
3.						
4.						
5.						
6.						
7.						
8.						
9.						
10.						

Total Points: _____

Railroad Review

Materials
• 4" soft foam or rubber balls

Objective
Students will review facts about building the Transcontinental Railroad or another important historical event they have studied.

Review is an important part of the learning process. How you conduct a review can make all the difference in whether or not students actually retain the information. Help students review *and* retain historical facts in this fun game of catch, which is adaptable to any unit of study.

1. Provide students with writing paper and pencils to review facts about a topic such as the Transcontinental Railroad. Have students draw a railroad track on their paper with ten rails going across the track.

2. As you review what students have learned about the topic, ask them to copy down ten facts on their paper, one fact on each rail of the track.

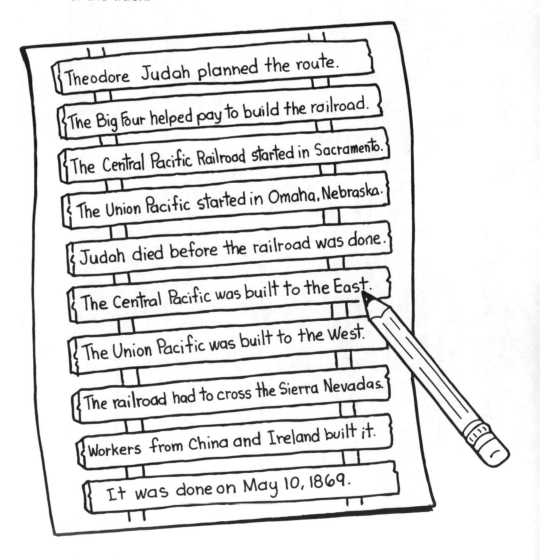

Theodore Judah planned the route.

The Big Four helped pay to build the railroad.

The Central Pacific Railroad started in Sacramento.

The Union Pacific started in Omaha, Nebraska.

Judah died before the railroad was done.

The Central Pacific was built to the East.

The Union Pacific was built to the West.

The railroad had to cross the Sierra Nevadas.

Workers from China and Ireland built it.

It was done on May 10, 1869.

3. Explain to students that they will play an outdoor game of catch to review what they have learned. Divide the class into teams of four, and then have those four students pair off (Team 1 and Team 2). Give each pair a ball and tell them to stand facing each other. Then ask each player to take ten giant steps backwards, so they are standing farther apart. Each player should have his or her paper listing ten facts and a pencil for keeping score.

4. Demonstrate how to play the game with three volunteers. The first player from Team 2 asks the first player from Team 1 a question based on a fact from the fact sheet. For example, if the fact is *Theodore Judah planned the route,* the question could be: *Who planned the route?* If the player from Team 1 answers correctly, Team 1 scores one point. The player from Team 1 then throws the ball to his or her partner. If the ball is caught successfully, Team 1 scores another point.

5. The player holding the ball takes one giant step closer to the middle. Now the second player from Team 2 asks the second player from Team 1 a question. After the question is answered, the second player from Team 1 tosses the ball back to his or her teammate. Each team can score up to four points on a turn.

6. The player holding the ball steps one giant step closer to the middle. Now it is Team 2's turn to score points. After demonstrating with a couple of questions, check that students understand how to play.

7. Invite students to play the game in their teams, while you watch and assist as needed. The game continues back and forth, one side moving one step closer to the middle after each toss. The game is over when the team members on one team are close enough to shake hands. The team with the most points wins the game.

8. After the game, ask students to share the most interesting fact they learned during the game.

Let's Draw!

Materials

- Let's Draw! Game Board reproducible
- video documentary or nonfiction picture book about Native American communities
- index cards
- sand timer
- die
- 2 game markers (e.g., pennies)

Objective

Students will review Native American communities and artifacts.

Most states in the United States have a rich history of Native American populations and communities. As you review these facts with students, use this game to help them identify specific objects found in Native American communities.

1. Distribute several index cards to each student. Watch a video documentary or read a nonfiction picture book to review what life was like in Native American communities long ago. Stop at key places and point out various objects found in the communities, asking students to identify their correct names (e.g., *hogan, salmon, weir, clay pot*). Instruct students to write down as many objects as they wish, one item per card. When students are finished, collect all the cards. Check over items on the cards and add more cards listing other objects you want students to review.

2. Tell students that they will play a game similar to the popular game *Pictionary*® (a registered trademark of Pictionary Incorporated) to help review what they've learned about Native American communities. A group of six to eight students can play at a time.

3. Reproduce a copy of the **Let's Draw! Game Board reproducible (page 80)** and laminate it for durability. Set up the game board for a group of students, and place the stack of index cards facedown beside the board. Set out two game markers, the timer, and a die. Group players into two teams and explain how to play the game while demonstrating with volunteers.

978-1-4129-5929-2

4. Both teams place their markers on *Start* and then begin the game by playing to see who gets control of the die. Each team chooses one player to draw the picture. These two players secretly look at the top card from the stack and read the word.

5. Start the timer. Both teams have one minute for the player to draw a picture of the word while teammates try to guess what it is. The first team to correctly guess the word takes control of the die. If neither team guesses the word before time is up, play is repeated using the next card in the stack.

6. The team that guesses the word rolls the die and advances their marker accordingly. (If they land on an unmarked space, they are the only ones who get to draw the picture and guess the word. If they land on a square with a pencil, both teams draw and play.) If the team guesses the word correctly, they roll the die again and their turn continues. If they do not guess correctly, the other team takes control of the die.

7. The other team must draw and guess a word correctly before they roll the die and advance their marker. If they are on a square with a pencil, both teams draw and play. The first team to reach *Finish* and guess their word correctly wins the game.

8. After all students have had a chance to play the game, allow time for students to reflect on the experience and discuss which words were easiest to guess and which were most difficult. Invite them to offer ideas that could help speed up the drawing process, such as using common symbols.

Extended Learning
Provide craft materials for each student to make a model of one object found in a Native American community. Invite the class to label and display their objects in a classroom museum.

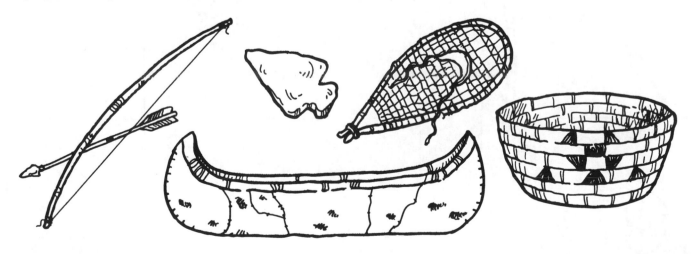

Let's Draw! Game Board

FINISH

START

CHAPTER 5

Physical Education, Art, and Music

Let's Walk!

Objective

Students will track the number of steps they walk, adding their mileage to their teammates' mileage until they reach a common goal.

Materials
- Walking Log reproducible
- Let's Walk Across Our State! certificate reproducible
- map of your state
- highlighter and markers
- pedometers
- small medals or trophies

Working with others toward a common goal can make physical fitness a lot more fun. In this activity, teams compete to be the first to walk enough miles to travel across their state from border to border. Individuals track their daily progress, adding their mileage to that of their teammates.

1. In preparation for this activity, determine how far you want students to walk during this game and how many days you want the game to last. Many fourth graders can walk about one mile in 10 to 15 minutes. Students will be keeping track of the number of miles they walk each day and adding these totals to their teammates' totals to discover the number of miles walked. The goal is for teams to collectively walk the distance from one end of the state to the other.

2. With these numbers in mind, locate an actual road route on a map of your state that crosses from border to border. Measure the number of miles it would take to travel this route from start to finish.

3. If your state is quite large (e.g., Texas or Alaska), you might want to organize your class into one entire team and compete against another class. Another option is to select a starting point and a stopping point within your state's boundaries. If your state is quite small (e.g., Rhode Island or Connecticut), you might choose to divide your class into two or three teams to compete against each other. Highlight the route students will be tracking with a highlighter.

4. Give each student a pedometer and show them how to use it. (If there are not enough pedometers, divide the class into pairs or small groups and give each group one pedometer. Instruct each of these groups to walk together.) Explain that students will use the pedometer to measure the distance they walk.

5. Tell students to count the number of steps they take and record their mileage on the days they walk. Show them the state map with the highlighted route, and explain that their goal is to add up the total number of miles it would take to walk along that route, from start to finish. Everyone gets a certificate when his or her team finishes the route, and the first team to finish earns a small medal or trophy.

6. Distribute copies of the **Walking Log reproducible (page 83)**. Demonstrate how to fill in the log at the end of each walking session, and add up the total number of individual miles as well as team miles.

7. Walk one lap together as a class around the playground or large gymnasium. Stop and check to see that students understand how to read their pedometers. Then have students walk on their own, staggering them to avoid crowding. After walking for a pre-designated time of 10 to 15 minutes, stop and return to class.

8. Tell students to check their pedometers and fill in their Walking Log according to the number of steps they took, the number of miles it equaled, and the total miles to date. Have them work together to add up the total miles for their team as well. Instruct students to record these numbers on their log.

9. Using a different color marker to represent each team, draw lines on the state map to represent each team's total mileage for that day. Each day your class walks together, fill in the Walking Logs and mark progress on the map.

10. As each team reaches the finish line, reward each student with a copy of the **Let's Walk Across Our State! certificate reproducible (page 84)**. For added fun, you may choose to award the first team to finish a small medal or trophy.

11. After your class has reached its goal, ask students to share their personal bests, such as the most miles they walked in one day. Discuss how walking is one of the best and easiest ways to stay physically fit.

Name _____ Date _____

Walking Log

Directions: Keep a record of how far you and your team walk each day.

Starting point: _____ Goal: _____

Total miles needed to reach our goal: _____

Date	My Steps Today	My Miles Today	My Miles to Date	Team's Miles Today	Team's Miles to Date

Let's Walk Across Our State!

Congratulations on walking enough miles with your team to cross our entire state!

Awarded to:

_____
(name)

_____
(date)

My team walked _____ miles!

Fill It Up!

Objective
Students will practice throwing and catching skills.

Materials
• buckets
• foam balls or tennis balls of two different colors
• chalk marker or cones

In this action-packed game, students progress toward health and fitness goals by honing throwing and catching skills. They will toss balls back and forth across the playing field to reach the teammate standing closest to an empty bucket. The first team to fill its bucket with balls wins the game.

1. Ask a pair of volunteers to demonstrate how to throw and catch a ball. Choose students who are athletically skilled and can give pointers to other students. Then divide the class into pairs and give them time to practice throwing and catching. Have them stand six to ten feet away from their partners as they toss the ball back and forth. Watch to see that students are practicing good form and motion.

2. Two teams of four students each are needed to play this game. Mark a playing field with a chalk marker or cones so students are standing across from each other, as shown in the diagram. On one side, starting with Team A, line up students side-by-side, three to four feet apart, *A, B, A, B*. Across from them, starting with Team B, line up students *B, A, B, A*.

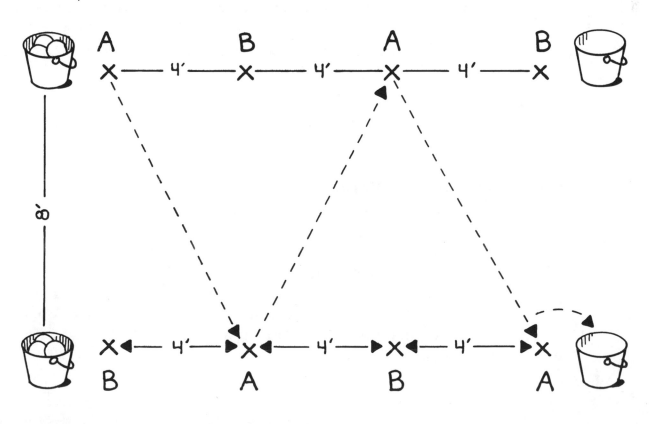

3. Place a bucket filled with ten tennis or foam balls next to the first member of Team A, and place an empty bucket at the other end next to the last member of Team B. Across the field, place a bucket filled with ten different-colored tennis or foam balls next to the first member of Team B, and place an empty bucket at the other end next to the last member of Team A.

4. After setting up balls and students as described, explain how to play the game. The game begins with the first player on both teams simultaneously tossing a ball diagonally across the field to the second player on their teams. When those players catch or retrieve the ball, they must return to their marked position before throwing the balls diagonally across the field to the next player, and so on, down the line. The last player catches the ball and places it in the empty bucket.

5. The first player must wait until the ball is in the bucket before throwing the next ball. The first team to fill its empty bucket wins the game.

6. After explaining the rules, demonstrate how to throw the ball diagonally from teammate to teammate across the field and down the line. Check to make sure students can easily identify who is on their team. Return the balls to the full bucket and start the game.

7. During the game, assist students as needed with throwing and catching the balls. Reinforce the need for good sportsmanship and team support. Invite students to cheer and encourage each other as they play.

8. After the game, ask volunteers to demonstrate skills they used to help them throw or catch the ball.

Extended Learning

Invite students to work with partners to practice their throwing and catching skills. First, have partners stand close together and toss the ball back and forth for one minute. Then have students take one step backward so they are standing farther apart. Instruct students to toss the ball back and forth again for another minute. Continue having them step farther and farther apart until they are about 15 feet apart. See how far students can move before throwing and catching the ball becomes too difficult.

Wacky Ball

Objective
Students will learn to successfully strike a ball with a racquetball racket.

Materials
- racquetball rackets
- tennis balls
- baseball diamond with backstop
- four bases

Baseball can be a frustrating experience for some students because of the challenge of hitting the ball. In this exciting game, students experience success as they hit a tennis ball with a racquetball racket, and then run around the bases to earn points for their team.

1. Before playing the game, ask which students have played on a baseball or softball team. Choose one or two volunteers to demonstrate how to hit a baseball.

2. Divide the class into two teams. Set up home plate and the three other bases, similar to a regular game of baseball. Position the first team behind the backstop. They will be first up to bat. Position the second team in the field. You will be the pitcher, unless you have a capable and willing student. (If a student pitches, be sure to stand behind the pitcher until the ball is hit. This will keep more aggressive outfielders from crowding home plate in anticipation of players who do not hit very far.)

3. Invite the first player up to bat. Demonstrate how to swing the racquetball racket to hit the tennis ball. Keep pitching to the student until he or she hits the ball. There are no foul balls, strike-outs, or walks in Wacky Ball. A ball hit in any direction is counted as fair.

4. As soon as the player hits the ball, he or she drops the racket and runs to first base. If the student safely reaches first base, he or she may continue running the bases until play is stopped. Play stops when someone in the outfield successfully throws the ball against the inside of the backstop. If he or she misses the backstop, the runner continues around the bases while the outfielders retrieve the ball and tries to throw it against the inside of the backstop.

5. Sometimes players will run past first base, second base, third base, home base, and on to first base again. Each base safely reached before the ball hits the backstop counts as one point for the team. Some players might earn up to ten points in one play!

6. Players who have already had a turn at bat stand behind the backstop with their teammates until everyone else on the first team has a turn. Then the teams switch places and the second team is up to bat. After each player on this team has a turn at bat, the game is over. The team with the highest score wins the game.

7. You may choose to allow only three or four students to "bat" before having teams switch places. This may create more interest and keep the game lively! Ask students which way they prefer to approach the game.

8. Provide students with tennis balls and racquetball rackets for independent practice. Encourage students to keep track of the number of points they score each time they play Wacky Ball, and challenge them to improve on their personal bests.

978-1-4129-5929-2

Whodunit?

Objective
Students will practice drawing portraits with correct facial proportions.

By learning proper facial proportions, students can gain confidence as artists and draw more realistic portraits. In this "crime-solving" game, students will collect clues about a suspect's facial features and practice drawing faces with proper proportions.

1. To prepare for the game, reproduce the **Whodunit? Game Cards reproducibles (pages 91–92)**. Copy a set of cards for each group of six students. Cut out the cards. On the back of each card, write the number shown on the opposite side (e.g., *1* for *hair*, *2* for *mouth*). Laminate the cards for durability, and then store each set in a resealable plastic bag.

2. Invite several volunteers to come to the board and draw a portrait according to your verbal instructions. Have students seated at their desks practice drawing as well.

3. First, tell students to draw an egg shape for the head. Describe proper facial proportions, allowing time for students to draw each feature. Tell students: *The eyes are halfway down the face. The bottom of the nose is halfway between the eyes and the chin. The mouth is halfway between the nose and the chin. The ears extend from the eyes to the bottom of the nose.* As you give instructions, walk around the room to check students' work. Use volunteers' examples from the board to point out the correct proportions.

Materials
- Whodunit? Game Cards reproducibles
- scissors
- resealable plastic bags
- dice
- drawing supplies

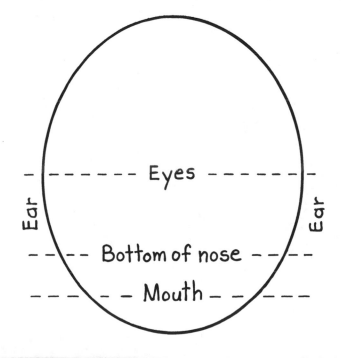

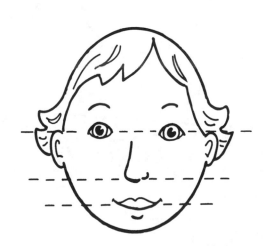

4. Tell students that they will play a detective game in which they practice drawing facial proportions to solve a crime. Start by asking who may have committed a silly, harmless crime such as: *Who turned off the lights? Who has the missing library book?* Tell students that their job is to collect clues about the criminal's description from eyewitnesses to the crime. They will then use these clues to draw a picture of the suspect.

5. Divide the class into groups of six players each. Give each group a die and a set of Whodunit? game cards. Have them place the cards facedown in six different piles. All the 1s go in one pile, all the 2s go in a second pile, and so on. Tell them to mix up (or shuffle) the cards in each pile. Then explain how to play the game.

6. Each player draws a large, egg-shaped outline of a person's head on a piece of paper. The first player rolls the die and draws the top card from the pile indicated on the die. This player then uses that clue to draw the facial feature of the suspect on his or her paper.

7. It is now the second player's turn to roll the die and pick up the top card from the corresponding pile. The second player uses that clue to draw the facial feature of the suspect on his or her paper. Play continues around the circle. If a player rolls a number for which he or she has already collected a clue, that player skips a turn. The first player to collect all six clues and complete the suspect's picture solves the crime and wins the game!

8. After the game, pair up students with partners. Instruct them to draw each other's portraits using proper facial proportions.

Whodunit? Game Cards

3 pointy ears **3**	**3** wide ears **3**	**3** flat ears **3**
3 small ears **3**	**3** medium ears **3**	**3** big ears **3**
2 small mouth, crooked teeth **2**	**2** medium mouth, missing top front tooth **2**	**2** big mouth, wearing braces **2**
2 small mouth, lips closed **2**	**2** medium mouth, lips closed **2**	**2** big mouth, lips closed **2**
1 boy with curly brown hair **1**	**1** boy with short, spiked hair **1**	**1** boy with shaggy blonde hair **1**
1 girl with straight blonde hair **1**	**1** girl with braids **1**	**1** girl with curly red hair **1**

Whodunit? Game Cards

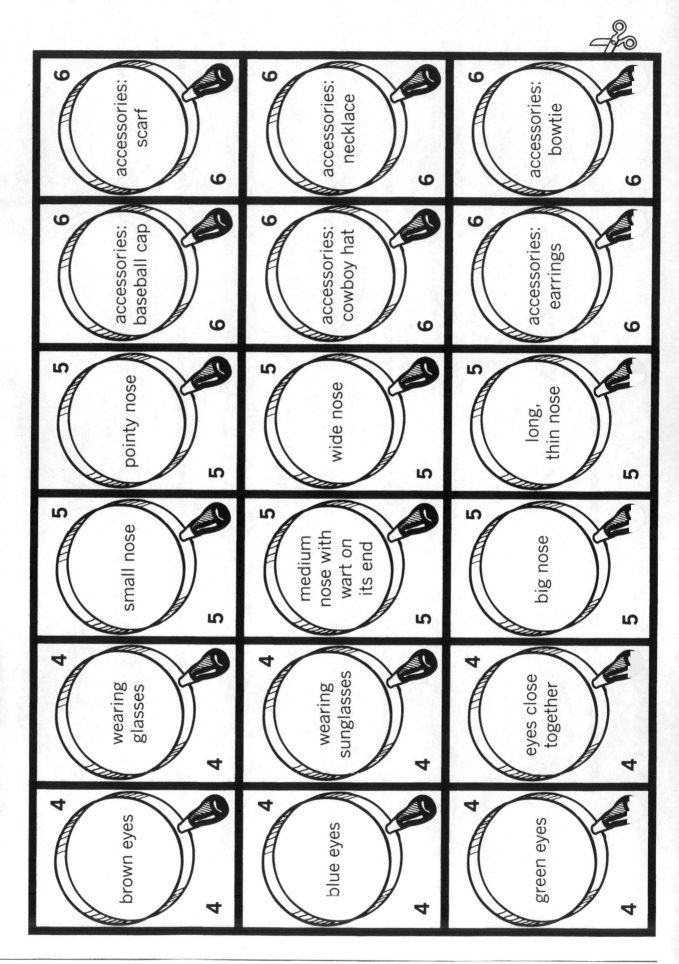

accessories: scarf — 6

accessories: necklace — 6

accessories: bowtie — 6

accessories: baseball cap — 6

accessories: cowboy hat — 6

accessories: earrings — 6

pointy nose — 5

wide nose — 5

long, thin nose — 5

small nose — 5

medium nose with wart on its end — 5

big nose — 5

wearing glasses — 4

wearing sunglasses — 4

eyes close together — 4

brown eyes — 4

blue eyes — 4

green eyes — 4

Reproducible

978-1-4129-5929-2 • © Corwin Press

Spot the Color

Objective

Students will become familiar with primary, secondary, and complementary colors on a color wheel.

Materials

- white paper plate
- chart paper
- crayons, markers, or paint, including primary colors (red, yellow, blue) and secondary colors (orange, green, purple)
- art supplies

Students love to experiment with color in their artwork. When they understand the concept of complementary colors, students will attempt to use interesting and evocative color combinations in pictures, paintings, and other artwork.

1. Prepare a simple color wheel to show to the class. Divide a paper plate into six equal, pie-shaped wedges. Starting in one space and moving clockwise, color or paint each wedge one of the following colors: red, orange, yellow, green, blue, and purple. Make sure that complementary colors are opposite each other on the wheel (i.e., red–green, blue–orange, yellow–purple).

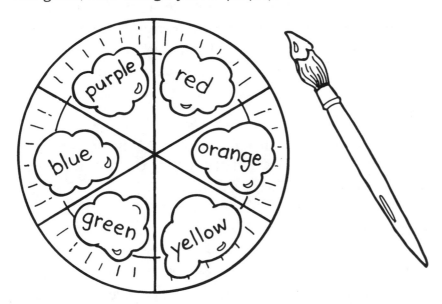

2. Show your color wheel to the class and point out the complementary colors. Explain that *complementary colors* are opposite each other on a color wheel. They are complementary because they have no primary colors in common. For example, blue and orange are complementary: orange contains red and yellow, but not blue. Tell students that when artists use complementary colors, their paintings exude high energy, tone, mood, and interest.

3. Provide art supplies to students. Instruct them to choose two complementary colors and use them to create a picture. Provide a couple of examples, such as red apples in a green tree, orange sunflowers in a blue vase, or a yellow duck with purple flowers.

4. Tell students that they will play a game similar to Four Corners to help them remember which colors are complementary. Paint a large red spot on a piece of chart paper. Repeat with blue, yellow, green, orange, and purple. Hang these signs around the room on the walls, copying their placement on a color wheel.

5. Then explain how to play the game *Spot the Color*. Choose one student to be the Caller and one student to be the Guesser. The Guesser sits down and closes his or her eyes. The Caller says *scramble*, which is the signal for students to move around and stand underneath the color spot of their choice. When the Caller says *freeze*, students must stay, or "freeze," in place.

6. Without peeking, the Guesser calls out one of the six colors. Whoever is standing next to that color's complementary color is out of the game. For example, if the Guesser says *red*, everyone standing next to the green spot is out of the game.

7. Practice one or two rounds before actually starting the game. Have everyone scramble and freeze as the Guesser calls out a color. Make sure students can identify the complementary colors and sit down accordingly. Then invite all students back in to play the game. The last two students still in the game become the new Caller and Guesser.

8. After the game, allow students to share their pictures with the class. Discuss how using complementary colors made their artwork stand out in interesting ways.

Extended Learning

Show students pictures of artwork created by famous artists such as Picasso, O'Keefe, Monet, Rembrandt, Gauguin, and Matisse. Invite students to point out primary, secondary, and complementary colors within the artwork. Ask them to describe the moods or feelings produced by different colors.

Classroom SuperStars

Objective

Students will improvise simple rhythmic and melodic variations on familiar songs.

Materials
• recordings of improvisational musicians such as Louis Armstrong or Ella Fitzgerald
• CD or cassette player
• camcorder and blank video or DVD

After watching television talent shows, many students want to be superstars. Invite them to become classroom superstars by staging their own talent show and learning about improvisation.

1. Choose one musician who was famous for improvising, such as Louis Armstrong or Ella Fitzgerald. Listen to samples of their music and ask students to point out rhythmic and melodic variations added to familiar melodies.

2. Demonstrate how to improvise by singing a familiar song with variations to the melody. Model how to change the rhythm by tapping a pencil, stomping your feet, snapping your fingers, or clapping your hands.

3. Divide the class into pairs and explain that they will play a game in which they compete to create their own musical improvisations. Ask each pair to choose one familiar song, practice singing the song with rhythmic or melodic variations, and prepare to perform. (You may choose to allow shyer students to use rhythm or musical instruments to improvise, rather than their voices.) Allow time for partners to practice. Check to make sure students are improvising.

4. Videotape each pair as they take turns performing for the class. When everyone is finished, watch the videotapes together. Encourage students to compliment and encourage each other's efforts.

5. Close the activity by asking students to vote for the pair of performers who improvised their song the best—your new Classroom Superstars! You may wish to award these students special prizes, such as homework passes or small treats. Make sure the whole class gets rewarded for their efforts as well.

References

Amethyst Galleries. (n.d.). *Amethyst Galleries' mineral gallery.* Retrieved May 6, 2007, from http://www.galleries.com/.

Beyers, J. (1998). The biology of human play. *Child Development, 69*(3), 599–600.

Color. (1992). In *Compton's encyclopedia* (Vol. 5, pp. 557–566). Chicago, IL: Encyclopedia Britannica, Inc.

Color Matters. (n.d.). *Color theory.* Retrieved May 6, 2007, from http://www.colormatters.com/colortheory.html.

Compass, magnetic. (1992). In *Compton's encyclopedia* (Vol. 5, pp. 622–623). Chicago, IL: Encyclopedia Britannica, Inc.

Continent. (1992). In *Compton's encyclopedia* (Vol. 5, pp. 687–692). Chicago, IL: Encyclopedia Britannica, Inc.

Gardner, H. (1983). *Frames of mind: The theory of multiple intelligences.* New York, NY: Basic Books.

Geometry. (1992). In *Compton's encyclopedia* (Vol. 9, pp. 73–80). Chicago, IL: Encyclopedia Britannica, Inc.

Jensen, E. (1995). *Brain-based learning and teaching.* Del Mar, CA: The Brain Store.

Lyman, K. (Ed.). (1986). *Simon & Schuster's guide to gems and precious stones.* New York, NY: Simon & Schuster.

McCarthy, B. (1990). Using the 4MAT system to bring learning styles to schools. *Educational Leadership, 48*(2), 31–37.

Minerals. (1992). In *Compton's encyclopedia* (Vol. 15, pp. 431–437). Chicago, IL: Encyclopedia Britannica, Inc.

Mountain. (1992). In *Compton's encyclopedia* (Vol. 15, pp. 633–636). Chicago, IL: Encyclopedia Britannica, Inc.

Oregon State University, Department of Geosciences. (n.d.). *Volcano world.* Retrieved May 6, 2007, from http://volcano.und.edu.

Railroad. (1992). In *Compton's encyclopedia* (Vol. 20, pp. 245–248). Chicago, IL: Encyclopedia Britannica, Inc.

Rock. (1992). In *Compton's encyclopedia* (Vol. 20, p. 85). Chicago, IL: Encyclopedia Britannica, Inc.

Tate, M. L. (2003). *Worksheets don't grow dendrites: 20 instructional strategies that engage the brain.* Thousand Oaks, CA: Corwin Press.

Volcano. (1992). In *Compton's encyclopedia* (Vol. 24, pp. 402–405). Chicago, IL: Encyclopedia Britannica, Inc.

Webster's new Riverside dictionary. (1984). New York, NY: Houghton Mifflin.

Wolfe, P. (2001). *Brain matters: Translating research into classroom practice.* Alexandria, VA: Association for Supervision and Curriculum Development.

Printed in the United States
By Bookmasters